Praise for

WHO WILL NAME THE BEES?

"Real and raw, this is a powerfully poignant collection of vignettes and poems that instantly draws the reader into the many facets of a mother-daughter relationship over a lifetime and through the ravages of Alzheimer's."

— DEBORAH RUDELL, AUTHOR OF *GRIT AND GRACE: THE TRANSFORMATION OF A SHIP & A SOUL*

"*Who Will Name the Bees* is a poignant memoir with a blend of pensive poetry and prose. It shows a daughter's love and devotion to her mother along with her ambition to keep her family stories alive. Meshed with humor amidst heartache, Sarah's voice is emotional and expressive."

— JENNIFER GASNER, AUTHOR OF *MY UNEXPECTED LIFE: FINDING BALANCE BEYOND MY DIAGNOSIS*

"This book gave me all the feels—tender moments, the all-too-familiar pain of losing a parent, hard life lessons, and shocking revelations—spanning childhood through adulthood. How do you wrap all of that into one? Enter storyteller Sarah Vosburgh. Beautifully written, this memoir lingers long after the last page—heartfelt, unforgettable, and absolutely worth reading."

— DR. RICHEL C. HORTINELA-DUDEN, PSYCHOLOGIST AND FELLOW BEEKEEPER.

"Reading this beautiful memoir, *Who Will Name the Bees* by Sarah Church Vosburgh, is sheer delight. Excellent writing, beautiful poetry dispersed in perfect places—this book has it all. Vosburgh's lyrical clear voice takes the reader on an incredible journey reflecting the power of that mighty force of helpless love we have for our mothers. I was mesmerized by the author's brilliant braiding of stories about her mother-daughter relationship that takes you from her childhood to the final days of her mother's life. This is a complicated and intense love story that will make readers laugh and, at times, cry. In the best books we learn something, we feel all the feels, and we reflect. This is one of those books. The best."

— LAURA L. ENGEL, AUTHOR OF *YOU'LL FORGET THIS EVER HAPPENED: SECRETS, SHAME, AND ADOPTION IN THE 1960S*

"Sarah Church Vosburgh's *Who Will Name the Bees* is a powerful memoir that follows the intense relationship between mother and daughter. It is moving in many unexpected ways. The story is simply gripping. I found myself flipping pages, unable to stop. And her poetry, dotted throughout each chapter, is lyrical and nearly spiritual "

— CARLOS DE LOS RÍOS, AUTHOR/POET OF *KIDS IN CAGES* AND WRITER OF THE FEATURE MOVIE *DIABLO*, STARRING WALTON GOGGINS AND DANNY GLOVER

WHO WILL NAME THE BEES?

A

MEMOIR

SARAH CHURCH
VOSBURGH

Helping talented writers publish exceptional books

This book is a memoir. It reflects the author's present recollecitons of experiences over time. Some names have been changed to protect privacy, some events have been compressed, and some dialogue has been recreated.

Who Will Name the Bees?
Copyright © 2025 Sarah Church Vosburgh. All rights reserved.

Printed in the United States of America. For information, address
Acorn Publishing, LLC
3943 Irvine Blvd. Ste. 218, Irvine, CA 92602

www.acornpublishingllc.com

Interior design by Nico Seidita
Cover design by Damonza

Anti-Piracy Warning: The unauthorized reproduction or distribution of copyrighted work is illegal. Criminal copyright infringement, including infringement without monetary gain, is investigated by the FBI and is punishable by up to five years in federal prison and a fine of $250,000.

All rights reserved. No part of this book may be used or reproduced in any manner whatsoever, including Internet usage, without written permission from the author.

AI Use Restriction: Without limiting the author's exclusive copyright, any use of this publication to train, develop, or improve generative artificial intelligence (AI) technologies, machine learning systems, or large language models is expressly prohibited. The author and Acorn Publishing LLC as the licensed publisher reserve all rights to license use of this work for such purposes.

ISBN-13: 9798885281478 (paperback)
Library of Congress Control Number: 2025919120

For my grandmother, the consummate storyteller; my mother, who engendered stories; and my daughters—lest ye forget.

Author's Note

This book is a work dealing with memory, reflection, and perception from the viewpoint of this author. It is based on actual events, but names, characteristics—including appearance and personal preferences, as well as identifying details—have been altered to protect individuals. In some cases, multiple people, places, or occurrences have been mashed into composite characters or updated for narrative flow. The perspectives are those of the author based on subjective experiences and memories with other interpretations as to the meaning and opinions of both events and persons described herein from other viewpoints. Any resemblance to actual persons, living or dead, outside the author's immediate experience, is coincidental.

Contents

To make a prairie (1755)

> To make a prairie it takes a clover and one bee,
> One clover, and a bee.
> And revery.
> The revery alone will do,
> If bees are few.

— EMILY DICKINSON

Prologue

If my relationship with my mother were a landscape, it would resemble an archaeological dig. Cordoned off, measured, recorded, and sifted through carefully for tiny traces of evidence of love. I *thought* I knew my mother loved me. It was just difficult to find proof. I became an expert excavator of the undemonstrative, mining little nuggets and finding them when I feared, on the brink of despair, there might be none.

My mother thought extending unconditional love to a small child would give rise to spoiled youth entitled to forgiveness, who clutched it to their puffed-up chests as a get-out-of-jail-free card. She said a child should never believe they were loved "no matter what." Some things were unforgivable, though I never knew what those might be. She felt the no-matter-what thing was permissiveness that could only lead to lawlessness both within the home and without.

Nor did she believe children should be primary in a mother's hierarchy when it came to love. Children, she said, should know a mother's love first went to her spouse. Her parents also required consideration. Children should be left to contemplate where they fell on the great mother's hierarchical table. A formation of conscience, she thought. The better behaved you were, the higher you hung on the chart.

Being an only child in this landscape with no one to scrabble against except my father (who held his place no matter how he behaved) and grandparents (with whom she fought on the regular) left me off-balance, trying to learn how best to behave, which turn of phrase or which look meant she loved me or was proud of me—neither of which were ever spoken to me or demonstrated, the latter so I'd not become conceited. I was left to excavate from the squares made by grid strings of a carefully plotted dig, the slivers of affection after each conversation, each event, each expression carefully sifted from surrounding silt in search of the elusive and highly valuable pottery shards.

"Was I good, Mommy?" I would ask. And my mother would reply, "I'll tell you when you've done something wrong. Don't beg for compliments."

I recall so distinctly searching for my parents' faces in the concert hall or on the bleachers for my recitals or games. They never came to games, yet I still looked. I guess that speaks volumes. They were always there for concerts, smack in the middle, my dad's arms folded over his chest, and my mom sitting prim and proper, back straight, hands nested in her lap, the two of them scowling like a suburban version of *American Gothic*, while other parents smiled and waved and chatted with one another.

I always felt stressed through the concerts, wondering what I had done to bring such antipathy to their faces. Afterward, while we ate requisite ice cream sundaes at the nearest shop, which they did dutifully with all the other families, they'd tell me about the students they thought had done well. I was never on the list. Even after solos. Compliments apparently spoiled children too. So it was, that I spent my part of my mother's life as an archeologist hunting for love, validation, and unconditional acceptance.

"Mother" Is a Four-Letter Word is the title of my mother's unwritten book. She complained vociferously during her lifetime that mothers were blamed for everything. Her relationship with

her own mother was tempestuous, but she gained some perspective on it over the years. When I complained that she fell short of my expectations during my childhood (cheeky little shit that I was), she threatened to write her own book and indicated it would be multigenerational. This was said in frustration and anger—or humor and jest—depending on backdrop. We shared many a laugh about it over my more mature years, noting events we thought should be included. It was both balm and amusement to any charged event. She swore me to secrecy over the title then, and I'm not sure how she'd feel about me sharing it now. I'm prepared for her to haunt me. She promised to do so anyway if I revealed her age. As it came to pass, she had no memory of any of it. My mother was the vessel for many of my stories, as mothers so often are.

My daughter the photographer tells me there is much nuance in photography, just like our stories. Each lens of a camera takes a different picture. The conditions or tools used during the shoot can change it. Sometimes, like our stories, we want our pictures sharp and focused; at other times, soft and diffuse. Sixty-odd years and various roles in life have given me understanding that I am not capable of truly representing another person. Those years have also taught me that my own observations and thoughts carry credibility. They can communicate beauty and complexity. We can't truly know another. We can't truly know ourselves. But this lack of omniscience does not invalidate the bits of knowledge and emotion we do have. So I tell stories. They are my armor against being swallowed by darkness for me and mine. They are my perspective, and mine alone. They are, in the end, a raw offering born of hope against the vastness of insignificance.

It's a human thing to ponder the meaning of life. I am not the only one to be made small by the emptiness and absoluteness of eternity and anonymity. Nor am I the only one to rail against it. I am, however, the only one who can tell the stories I tell herein. It is my own paltry effort to avoid *not* our primordial collective fear of death, but our fear of not having mattered. My mother mattered.

Growing up, I knew very little about who my parents had been before I was aware of being me. Self-awareness allowed me a window on who they were after my life began in the self-centered manner of all children, and later in the self-centered manner we cannot avoid because we are human and our perspective is limited. Of course, I heard stories—the oral family history about bits of my parents' childhoods, and their courtship and marriage. I had an album of pictures from their wedding and a paucity of pictures from their childhoods. Some of the photographic record is lost or dispersed. Most of it doesn't exist, either due to poverty or scarceness of materials—especially silver—during World War II.

I loved the stories, though. Begged for them to be told and re-told. I loved hearing different people's versions of the same tale. There were not a lot of them. This was due partly to a lack of exposure to my dad's side of the family, and partly to both families' private nature. I was young when I figured out there were major gaps and began asking questions. Sometimes I got a response. Other times I was told it was none of my business, that some things were better left in the past, or that there was no recollection. Lack of recollection would be a foreshadow.

Collecting stories became a passion. My own, my family's, and those I heard or experienced in the company of friends and neighbors. It wasn't long before it occurred to me that I was meant to be the keeper of stories for my family, and in some cases unintentionally for my friends and their families. It took much longer to fathom the dichotomy of burden and honor in that responsibility.

One of my deepest fears is memory loss. This fear isn't irrational. I watched first my grandmother and later my mother lose their memories and their very essences to Alzheimer's.[1] I

---

1. Alzheimer's consumes a large portion of public health spending and is a

suspect my great-grandfather was likewise afflicted from stories my mother told of his wildly inappropriate behavior (public nakedness, incoherent babbling, word salad, and breast-grabbing) and her desperately trying to mucilage his shoes to the floor as a little girl when she was tasked with watching him in his dotage so he wouldn't wander from their home. I am left with their stories and my experiences to share forward. A daunting task as I try to make my own mark.

It isn't just about memory for me but the whole of memory, not cherry-picked memory. I long ago grew weary of the *don't-speak-ill-of-the-dead* elevation to sainthood that seems to accompany a passing. This has been a source of anger and resentment for me. It's as though the person who died wasn't good enough, so we must sanitize and embellish their life to make it palatable to those who would listen to their stories. It dims their character and abrades their facets, leaving them flat and uninteresting.

I have no desire to be cleansed. I am who I am, and I would like to be represented as such if anyone cares to speak of me after I'm gone. Much like artwork, our actions, words, and very selves are different things to different people. We've little control over how others see us or how they may interpret our intentions.

That said, there are truths. The stories, and *my truths* herein, are a talisman against the ravages of Alzheimer's hanging from our family tree.

---

substantial and growing burden on public healthcare. Costs are expected to exceed one trillion by 2050. Annual new US dementia cases are projected to double from about 514,000 in 2020 to one million by 2060. (National Institute on Aging, 2024)

October

Love, Lies, and Rocking Chairs

There were no black eyes or other obvious bruises when she answered the door, though her blouse was buttoned askew, her hair looked like she'd combed it with an eggbeater, and her eyebrows and widow's peak had been filled in with black marker. Lord knows what else she'd gotten into. Always clumsy, my mother often had bruises, though they'd been increasing of late. The creep (husband)—was nowhere to be found, for which I was simultaneously grateful and perturbed. Grateful she'd been allowed to complete her morning ablutions in peace; annoyed with myself for not planning to be there early enough to help her prepare because I thought *he* would. Independently preparing to go out was a given for an adult. That worked until it didn't. Never mind. Focus on her. Lie to her. Make this happen quickly. Get her out of here to safety. Little did I understand the relative nature of safety.[1]

"Hi! Fancy seeing you here!" For a lifetime my mom had trouble attaching names to faces. This was her typical greeting to

---

1. A version of "Love, Lies, and Rocking Chairs" was first published in *Shaking the Tree: Brazen. Short. Memoir (Vol. 2): Things We Don't Talk About* edited by Marni Freedman and Tracy J. Jones, published by MCM Publishing, 2020

buy herself time to search her memory banks, and my cue as a child not to ask. Today she was searching for *my* name.

"We have a date today, Ma."

"We *do*?"

She greeted me with an uncharacteristic hug that morning. I hugged gently back; she seemed so small and frail. "I've learned to hug; I guess people don't know you care unless you do" was what she had told me growing up, while withholding hugs from me but sharing them with others when she thought it socially advantageous. No worry, her hugs were awkward, stiff, a bit too long, and a bit too tight. Her hug this day was my cue to tell the lie I had prepared that in retrospect I probably didn't need, but I still saw her as capable of so much. I told it with equal measures of angst and self-loathing.

"We're headed to Countryside Care today, remember? You need to get your blood pressure under control, and they need a florist to teach flower arranging."

"You're coming too?"

"Yes, I'm gonna stay for a bit, but then you'll have work to do."

"But you'll come back to get me?"

"I will be back."

Looking into the confused, fearful face of my mother, whose eyes nevertheless held hope, I had never felt more unlovable and less trustworthy. It had taken weeks of planning—and many white lies—to lead to this mockingly beautiful day with a sky the color of my dad's silk screen inks labeled "cerulean." Vivid crimsons, yellows, and oranges, of a New England autumn completed the scene, which hadn't a care for our drama or the protective necessity of closing off my heart so I could survive the blackness playing out in my mother's life. There was no hope now. No turn toward the future where there might be even a suggestion of hope for improvement or a twinkle of joy in recognition. We'd entered a one-way dark, spikey cave where the entryway behind sealed us into darkness with no exit light beckoning ahead.

We were on our way to the memory support facility—misnomer that it is—and I had told the first of many sets of lies to get my mother in the door. The one-way door which she would enter and never return from. After this she would never again cuddle at night with her kitty, or make herself a cup of coffee and forget where she'd put it, or curl up in the reading chair in her library with the newspaper, or spend an afternoon in her gardens, or soak in a tub full of lavender bath salts to relax and wash away her cares, or shuffle down the hall to her bedroom closet to find her favorite sweater against a chill that wasn't there, or answer the door delighted to see the faces of her granddaughters—taller than she, whose names she could not remember—with her bra on over two sweatshirts.

This particular morning came after weeks of paperwork and an interview held at a local restaurant, else she'd not have gone. They'd called me after the interview, which had included the creep.

"Hello?"

"Hi, this is Countryside Care memory care unit calling. We interviewed your mother today, and we have some concerns."

"That you can't take her in memory care"

"No, we think she's a *perfect fit*, but we don't think we should wait until next month. We'd like to skip her up on the waiting list and have her move in next week."

"Next week?"

"Yes. When she was interviewed today, we noticed her husband talked with his hands quite a bit, and every time he raised them your mother leaned away and cowered in her seat. The social worker noticed bruises, too, that we think are suspicious. We think he may be abusing her."[2]

The pit of guilt and anger in my stomach grew and threatened to exit in projectile fashion. They wanted to move up her admit-

____

2. Emotional and relational effects include ambiguous loss, guilt, stress, and shifts in family roles. (CDC, 2024)

tance for her safety. Here I was, working desperately to help my mother maintain her independence, thinking she had the support of someone who claimed to love her, only to find out that frustration had potentially gotten the better of him and she was at the battered, bruised, black-eyed end of it.

In preparation for this day I'd known was coming (though not quite so soon), I had begun pulling favorite items from her laundry for the past several weeks to hang in her small closet in her small room. She would be the teeny-tiny woman in the teeny-tiny room with the bare necessities; a single bed, night table, reclining chair, and small bathroom with a shower. I could count the number of times my mother had taken a shower on one hand. She preferred baths. This small fact tortured me. She sang in the bathtub, her clear straight tone giving voice to spirituals and folk songs. She always came out renewed and refreshed. The facility didn't have bathtubs.

After the phone call, I went into full gear. I told the creep that the date had been moved up. He expressed sadness but did not ask why. I took knickknacks and blankets and artwork from her home I thought would provide comfort and familiarity in her new surroundings. He did not participate. I bought new sheets for the single bed with Snow White (Disney) on them, because these days it was a movie she loved to watch over and over. It led to conversations like:

"Do you know what I saw in the backyard?"

"No Ma, tell me."

"It was so cute; there was a mommy bear sitting under the apple tree feeding her baby an apple. He was taking bites as she held it for him, and all the raccoons, and deer, and birds, and little mice were there eating grains and seeds I left out for them. It was an animal party, right in my backyard!"

∼

I arranged for flowers to be delivered weekly to her room for her night table, and a monthly seasonally-related wreath for her door. I had to get special permission from memory care. But unlike the other plain doors with institutional nametags on them, hers would be discernable immediately to her and I hoped, to others whose company she would come to enjoy. In my search for an appropriate facility, I ran into two old ladies from church—I had wondered where they'd gone off to. The same fate, I guess. Familiar faces—not that it would make a difference for my mom, who on a good day in her youth had trouble recalling faces.

Mom was glad to see me when I arrived to pick her up that day. Even though she didn't recognize me, she knew I was familiar and trustable. I took full advantage of her trust and joy. She couldn't remember where we were going or what we were doing. So I spun the tale. Lies rolled off my tongue in simple language as though she were the child whose short stature she had. I reminded her it was critical to get her blood pressure under control, and I thought a stay at this place would be preferable to time in the hospital, which the doctor had said (lie) would be necessary in order to find a way to regulate her pressure. In addition, the facility needed someone to do workshops for the "old folks" on flower arranging (lie)—and she was just the florist to do it. She was not one of "them" at seventy-something, of course, still only admitting to being forty. She had been a sought-after presenter at garden clubs, junior leagues, and libraries on flower-arranging just a few years before. At this point she could barely keep a conversation going for three exchanges on most days, let alone plan to teach others.

"But my blood pressure is fine! Why do I have to do this?"

"Because it's only fine sometimes. The rest of the time it's dangerously high."

"No! It's fine."

"Okay, but doctor's orders."

"My life is not my own."

Indeed, her life was no longer her own. *How is it she remembers and holds on to stuff when I need her to forget?*

I repeated the lie so often, so lovingly and carefully, that I almost believed it myself. She bought it with reticence for the time necessary to get her in the door and meeting folks, mostly because she was distracted by the opportunity to spend time with me even though she didn't remember my name or our connection.

They told me to stay only as long as necessary. I wasn't to help her find her room or tell her about the creature comforts I had painstakingly assembled for her. No, I was to introduce her to the head nurse and the director whom she had already met but did not recall, perhaps facilitate getting her involved in an activity, and sneak away. I was to abandon my mother without even a goodbye. The latter I did not do. I let her know I was leaving and said I would be back. I implied I'd take her with me (lie), though I never said so. I just let her think it, if she could think that far. A sin of omission, another prevarication.

My formerly fierce, smart, competent mother looked at me in that moment with a mixture of acquiescence, dread, and confusion, and an unexpected but distant twinkle of recognition in her eyes. How could a look from this tiny woman who couldn't remember her husband's name hold so much?

"I love you, sweetheart. See you in a little while."

"I love you too, Mom."

The resignation, acceptance, and love hit me at that moment. I had finally spoken the stark and solid truth as I turned my back and walked away. And this—the naked, sparse truth—felt like the other lies.

My shoulders slumped in defeat and an effort to protect my heart. One foot moving mechanically in front of the other, I'm not sure how I made it out the doors to the parking lot or remembered where I left the car. Memories flooded my thoughts, vying for position like squabbling siblings. They were overwhelming and had an element of vertigo, my world spinning and swirling as though I was caught in a vortex of time. My efforts to calm down and reassure myself that I'd done the good and right thing were feeble against the cacophony of self-criticism.

How could you take her like this from all she knows? How could you lie? How could you not manage a 4'11" old woman in your own spacious home? Remember when you broke her favorite record? Remember when you didn't thank her for the dress she made you? Remember when you told her you went to the library and didn't? Remember when you wouldn't tell her you loved her? Remember when you didn't make honors? How could you?

I tried to slow my breathing, and I became aware of warmth in the closed car on this brisk, clear day. The toastiness and eventual slowing of my breathing brought on tears, and I sat and sobbed. A child's sob where ribs are sucked inward and breath comes in shuddering, desperate gulps against pain.

Spent and exhausted, I gave in to the memories and drove home, my mind still in rapid random playback. In the living room, I dropped into my favorite chair, an old black Hitchcock rocker given to my parents as a wedding present by a favorite auntie. As pieces like this do, it made its way to our home when our first was born.

Traditional, it had a subdued gold design of a cornucopia of fruits and flowers on the top section that secured the back rails. This had been worn away in the center down to the wood from the many times a head had rested against it. I don't recall it ever looking any other way. I remember running my fingers over that section as a child in awe of the wear it sustained in our small family life. I cannot look at it or sit in it now without the evocative presence of my mother. Today is no different and another memory comes rushing forward, pushing the others aside.

Too big to sit in my diminutive mother's lap in the rocker, I pad into her bedroom in my footed yellow pajamas after a nightmare about challenging a wicked witch behind the tulips in our backyard. I crawl up as she lays her book aside and wraps her arms around my fearful self. For me at that time those arms could've held and steadied the world, which she had taught me was "so big it took a whole day to turn around once." In this memory, those arms hug me tightly, as much to keep me from slipping as to be close in her tiny lap. I was still young enough that hugs would not spoil me. I am warm and safe with my ear against her chest. Sleepy and secure while I listen and feel the hum of her sweet alto singing her favorite spiritual, "Swing Low, Sweet Chariot."[3] I am loved and protected, with not a care in the world. I am held and sung to with aching tenderness by a little but fierce Shakespearean protector.[4]

What a staggeringly, hauntingly precious gift from a mother to a developing child. The tears begin again. This time they are quiet and relentless with acceptance and loss. Truth. Finally, a truth.

---

3. Horace Clarence Boyer, ed., "Swing Low, Sweet Chariot." *Lift Every Voice and Sing II.* Church Publishing Inc., 1993
4. William Shakespeare, *A Midsummer Night's Dream*, act III.

Sugaring Devotions

Relentless heartbeat of autumn axe
energy stacked and stashed.

Revisited as days begin to lengthen
anticipation of golden goodness

While earth lies fallow
I'm out, about, full buckets, crisp snow, blinding Lauds.
Gardener friends itch inside
perennial frustration and longing,

As I split logs, bank fires, celebrate Maples
who offer lifeblood and sweeten The Hours.

White smoke rises and neighbors know by Vespers
to mosey over with cups and draw off warmth and strength of
Communion.

The Catechism or Confraternity of Christian Doctrine

It was another beautiful autumn day in another time, and the hilly and winding road my mother and I were traveling evoked awe in the way one might expect in a cathedral, the patches of blue peeking through the leaves in a canopy reminiscent of stained-glass windows. The road was an old Pony Express route the locals called "the mountain." It was not a mountain, but it was the highest peak in the vicinity. It was a dangerous road, especially in inclement weather. It had one lane each way and very little shoulder. The trees were almost close enough to touch from the car, and the road meandered, with many blind curves. In later years, prior to her captivity, my mother would leave home on foot to walk this road to "get home," only to be found confused and disoriented by a family friend, who would bring her back to her husband, who seemed unconcerned and unaware she had even left.

On other drives we had stopped—dangerously—many times on this road to dig up wild daylilies or Queen Anne's lace. To go "over the mountain" was to take a long (well, ten-minute) and arduous trip up and over into the "wilds" on the "other side." To say you were going "over the mountain" was to indicate a significant event and commitment as all that was necessary for life could be found in our own community on the "civilized" flats at the foot of "the mountain."

It was the sixties and we were in my mother's ancient clunker of a convertible that she'd had since before marriage. It was the color of a baby's first poop and had huge back fins and a dirty, faded white top that ached and groaned and dropped all manner of dust when asked (manually) to fold down. This day was too cold for that. We were on the downhill of our return trip "over the mountain" when the car gave a cough and a lurch, and we were suddenly limping along to a truck stop tucked into the trees.

"Well," she said, "we'll have to hoof it home or to a phone booth, whatever comes first."

"Okay, Mommy."

"Remember," she added, "we're never supposed to be with a man we don't know."

Truckers, along with a list of many other folk, were not to be trusted, and one should never be alone with them. Plumbers, electricians, gas station attendants, the meter men, the ice cream truck kids, the men who filled the gumball machine at the grocery store with their dirty hands—which is why I could never get a gumball—all men, all dangerous. Men were dangerous. And germy.

Walking downhill on this hazardous route was far more dangerous than meeting any trucker, but my mother was steadfast. We must keep moving and reach a phone to call my father (a safe man) or the garage for a tow (where we knew the man, and men we knew were sort of safe, unless they showed up in the wrong place where we didn't know them). When driving "the mountain" road, at one point downhill toward home, there was a short window where all of the city, the riverbanks, and the suburban surrounds opened up fleetingly through the landscape.

"Mommy, lookit the city! You can see it longer when we're walking."

"Mm-hmm, you can."

"And lookit all the colors, Mommy, and how blue the river is!"

"Mm-hmm, 'tis very pretty."

"And it smells so nice out here, all the fall smells. Someone has a fire; it smells so good."

I think she was surprised I wasn't complaining. Who would complain, though, with such a view? And who would complain when they knew their mother was living vibrating anxiety and fear? It rolled off her like a deep foreboding fog. I was only marginally successful at distracting her from it.

A man pulled over in front of us and waited for us to reach his car. He offered a ride. In his suit and tie, he didn't look like a truck driver—but he could be lying, and we didn't know him, and bad men lie. My mother would not take a ride from a strange man, thank you very much. He may as well have been one of those terrible truckers. Despite her stilettos and my sturdy, functional Mary Jane school shoes, we trudged on in our quest for the bottom of the mountain. Luckily for the blisters forming on my heels, another man pulled over. He recognized me from catechism, and I recognized him and his car from the pick-up line after our Wednesday afternoon classes. His daughter and I were friends once a week in that Confraternity of Christian Doctrine tutelage. We would be confirmed together. A "nice Catholic man," and he probably didn't even know how to drive a truck. He knew no one would be walking that particular road by choice, especially with a child. We chatted about school and CCD, and my heels rejoiced.

I don't remember getting home or even what happened to the car, though I think we traded it shortly thereafter. I do remember the sights and smells of that day in my favorite season, and one of my mother's rare compliments: "I'm proud of you, Gremlin; you made the best of a bad situation."

Who Taught You?

In yet another October in the aughts, my mother would become a teacher in our homeschool. By then, I was married with two young daughters, and we lived on a lake. However wonderful the colors were at that time of the year, they were doubly so at the lake, their reflections sparkling on the water in all their splendor. The girls delighted in this time of year, and in Gran's visits every Tuesday for a morning of art lessons, lunch, and an afternoon of reading and math lessons. They loved asking questions about when she or I had been young students.

"Who taught you to read, Mama?" asked my emergent reader.

"Gran did."

"Did she homeschool you?"

"I went to public school. Gran taught me before I went to kindergarten. She wrote books for me."

The time and effort my mother had devoted to preparing me for school yielded fun when I was a child, and awe as I looked back as an adult for how she managed with a full-time job. Handwritten books with her own illustrations or pictures cut and glued from magazines. My informal early education was a labor of love.

For the beginning of her educational career, my mother was a teacher. She taught first and then sixth grade. She talked about teaching and students at the dinner table, and I always went to school with her in August to help set up her classroom, even as a very young child. She told stories of leaving bags of clothing or groceries on porches in the dark of night, all stealth on her mission to aid families who were struggling with the necessities. She worked at home almost every night on lesson plans or corrections. She set a phenomenal example of a work ethic and caring as I was growing up.

Many of the children in our community were homeschooled in the early aughts, and my daughters were enamored of the idea. They were already in school and saw many of the neighbor kids on a more relaxed schedule. My children longed for it. They both hated school for different reasons. Having hated school myself, and not wanting them to endure the same misery, I finally gave in to homeschooling over a summer when the begging was relentless, and the previous year had yielded little learning. My kids didn't know what they were getting into though. I'm a teacher too. There would be lessons, and schedules, and high expectations for more than a year's growth in a year's time. Being a public school-teacher herself, my mother was skeptical of the whole business but embraced it with both arms when I asked her to help.

"I'd love to help. If anyone can do this successfully, you can. You're a better teacher than I ever was."

Such praise from my mother was almost nonexistent. I had never known she thought that. It went straight to my heart for safekeeping. I gave her a choice of subject matter. She chose art. My mother was talented artistically, quite proficient in sketching and watercolors, and would be the perfect person to share her ability as well as her joy. She planned lessons and consulted me on them, working and reworking them so that she was sure her charges would feel successful and learn. She asked what their reading lessons were so she could include vocabulary and phonics in her art lessons. A true master.

The girls loved it. Gran spent the whole day with us on Tuesdays. She came early for breakfast to cook with them and followed the directions the children gave her from their written recipes—what better way to practice reading, math, and organization? My daughters introduced her to mise en place, which was a new concept for her. She split up reading and writing lessons with me in the afternoons, and did her complimentary art lesson in the morning. I watched her work her magic and still couldn't tell you how she taught them perspective and value and shading at such young ages. I often did their lessons right alongside them, not wanting to pass up on the chance to be her student again. The three of them always had a finished piece. Mine always looked worse than theirs did.

My first and third graders often met their gran on Tuesday mornings dressed in costumes so they could act out plays they invented for her at lunchtime. I did their hair as they requested, Lillie with blonde ring curls that made a golden halo, Helen in an almost black plait or banana curl that reached her hips. Dressing up for Gran was important.

"Mama, will you fix my hair? Gran is coming today! Put in lots of pretties, okay?"

During all this, my girls asked for stories about how Gran had taught me to read and write and cipher. I didn't learn well in school in my elementary years—I don't know why—but my mother made sure I had the skills I needed, and she did it without me really knowing it was happening. I remember a few instances, but I think she worked her magic into the mundane and I never saw it coming. The girls loved this notion, that my mother was a teacher in my school. Their favorite story in those hours, with our three generations together in homeschool, was the story about me learning to write.

"Who taught you to write, Mama?"

"Gran did."

"How did she teach you?"

My mother taught me to write by trusting me to think and express my own thoughts. I would go to her with a long explanation of something I wanted to say that I'd been pondering for an assignment and looking for "better words" to express it.

"How do I say that, Ma?"

"The way you just told me."

It became a joke in the kitchen schoolroom on days she would be there. The girls delighted in giving her an endless explanation of something they wanted to write, and then ask:

"How do I say that, Gran?"

"The way you just told me."

"Aahhhh! But I don't remember what I said."

"Never mind! You thought of it once; you can think of it again."

After lessons was lunch, taken lakeside if weather permitted. There they would banter with her about flowers and fishes and bugs, how mean the swans were, and the aerie nearby. There were more lessons, and days ended with a read-aloud. My mother read books beyond their reading levels, novels like *Black Beauty* and *Little Women,* or biographies of composers and artists. When each tome was completed, she would gift them the copy from her own library to add to their growing library so they would have it to read again. When she had a house fire years later, these were the only books that survived from her original collection.

We only homeschooled for two years. These days, looking back, my daughters will say that many, if not most, of their memories of my mother, their gran, were tinged by her memory failings, but these homeschool memories stand out, crystal clear, sparkling, and colorful like the reflections of autumn colors on the lake.

November

The Phone to Nowhere

My mother's scenery had been pruned and smoothed by now, and the path she navigated was narrow and claustrophobic. Were she to reach for branches of memories and associations, she would meet only with a glassy smooth high wall upon which she could not gain purchase, nor could she scale it. The sky above was a mockery of the understanding she could not reach; the path at her feet was slick and uncompromising.

The insidiousness of this disease allowed for random automatic behaviors to rise to the surface and become compelling, even perseverative. Such was dialing the phone. Before her incarceration, she had engaged in what my husband Brodie and I referred to as "dialing for dollars." She would hunt for the phone, which was hidden from her, and dial random numbers in an attempt to reach someone. When she hit pay dirt, she would beg whomever she reached to come get her because there was a strange man in her house. At this point in time, she often did not recognize her husband or his voice. This would result in a house call from the police (not necessarily a good use of their time when she had a caretaker) and an admonishment to keep the phone from her. No easy task.

Upon her entry into the memory unit, I was asked if my mother would have her own phone. Given her dollar dialing, I thought it best she not have one. So I cut her off from the world, and from her friends and experiences, helping to polish the glassy walls cloistering her. Silly me, I assumed that would be the end of the problem. Isolate her and all would be well.

Not so fast. Nope. She was still in there. She may not have been able to reach up and out of the brambles of her mind, but she was able to sleuth around and soon discovered other folks had phones in their rooms. Unable to remember my dad was long gone, she could still reach for a twig of memory. She simply slipped into other rooms and made desperate calls to her home number, which had been the same her whole adult life. Assuming it was my father she reached, she would leave a message or ask whoever answered to pick her up because she was "ready to go home now." They were dark, pitiful, and plaintive cries for rescue. The husband never listened to the messages. Each time she called, he hung up when he recognized her little voice on a live call and then called us to complain. I judged him for this only to find myself doing it later, tears replacing complaints.

So began the slow march toward her expulsion from the unit —something I hadn't even contemplated. I figured she was in the memory unit, and safe, and even if she required more involved levels of care, she would stay at the facility. They had other protocols apparently, though they'd never been discussed with me. They were building a case for her expulsion from school. She wasn't adjusting. She couldn't be controlled. She was awake at night, soldiering around, looking for staff to chat up. She was rarely settled during the day, looking around furtively for phones and heaven knows what else. This they found unacceptable. She was breaking basic privacy rules that all the other residents— regardless of their memory status—seemed able to follow. She needed constant attention to maintain quiet behavior. The memory care gatekeepers called me each time she was annoying them. I was confused and frustrated by this. Were she a child in preschool or grade school, we would be helping her make the adjustment.

"Your mother is not adjusting well."

"What can be done to help her?"

"Well, we expect her to be socially integrative."

"What do you mean by that?"

I knew what they meant; I'd used the phrase "socially integrative" countless times myself, but not without enumerating a history of attempts to help or a plan to help going forward.

"Does anyone redirect her?" I wondered aloud.

"Ma'am, we haven't the time for that.[1] She needs to do this on her own."

We got her a phone, hoping it would help. It was placed on her nightstand, and she was able to dial whenever she chose. It was rigged so that she would get a dial tone and, after any ten numbers and requisite rings, she would reach a voicemail greeting. It was one we had from before my dad had died since his was the voice she recalled, not remembering the creep at all. My husband set it up to direct the caller to leave a message, which was followed by the requisite beep. It did not record her ramblings.

Well, it did initially, but self-preservation changed that. I, too, couldn't bear her rambling, abject cries for help. This way, I didn't have to listen to the anguish in her isolation. (How do families do this?) Once she left her message, she would be satisfied for a time and go about the business of packing or waiting by a door, any door, dressed, with lipstick askew, and black indelible marker— that she managed to squirrel away from the nurses' station— coloring her gray hairs, for my dad to pick her up. Until she forgot and started all over again, making a call on the phone to nowhere. Some days I would stop by for an afternoon visit, and she would exclaim: "I'm so glad you're here; I've been calling you all day."

---

1. Skilled nursing facilities cost families 95–108 thousand dollars/year on average. Alzheimer's Association. "Long Term Care Options." Accessed October 4, 2025. www.alz.org/help-support/caregiving/care-options/long-term-care.

As my mother began the settling-in process, I had high and unrealistic hopes she would be happy. To make for a better transition to the facility, it was recommended we not visit for the first week to ten days and then visit only a couple of times the two weeks after. This was against my better judgement, but these folks did this for a living, and I felt it important to trust their expertise.

The prescribed adjustment period would bring our family to just before Thanksgiving. I would be happy to have my mother home for that holiday, whatever her state of mind. So I passed the time with the romance of how happy she would be to eat food she loved and celebrate this cherished tradition in our family. She had always enjoyed Thanksgiving, especially after we had taken to hosting. The plan was that my hostess responsibilities would be seen to by my tween daughters, and I would guide her through the day. I had a healthy dose of trepidation about managing her—she could become prickly when she felt left out or found herself in an unfamiliar situation—but for the larger part I looked forward to all of it.

Back at the ranch, they were collecting evidence of her inability to adjust: her phone calls, her nighttime sojourns, and the quickly scribbled note she had left by her phone requesting help on the pad I thought would be a good idea to leave for her (with silhouettes of kittens on it because she loved cats). She always had a pad and pencil at the ready.

Mom, Dad, please come. Life here is becoming impossible, depressed—please come get me. Please.

As it was, they told us shortly before Thanksgiving that my mother was not adjusting sufficiently to her new environs to allow a break from the routine she had not yet internalized, and they suggested we not bring her home for the holiday. There was bottomless guilt in the relief she would not have to be watched every second, guided through every moment, and have most conversations explained to her—and still be met with a blank stare. There was also bottomless sorrow, and a sense of missed opportunity to make the best of The Last Thanksgiving.

What I could have done differently, I don't know. If I had realized it were the last, I would have been sad to the point of ruining everyone else's day, which neither I nor my mother would have wanted. As it so often is, we don't know when the last thing is to be. A hug, an affirmation, an acknowledgement, a dinner, an argument—it matters not. We haven't the opportunity or foreknowledge to celebrate or mark every "last" that happens in our lives.

There would be an empty chair at the table. I accepted her absence reluctantly and set my sights on Christmas.

Fourth Grade

Snow Day

The snow was white
Oh, what a sight!
The trees were bare
Without a care
I made cakes with snowy white flakes
The sky was gray
Oh, what a day!

The Car to Nowhere

It was a blessing that my mother became increasingly more willing to have folks drive her from one place to another. She had been an overly cautious—even anxious—driver her entire life. This made for constant switching from gas to brake to gas, such that she challenged her passengers' neck muscles. She braked at green lights and in intersections, and she took turns wide and painfully slowly. There were honks and squealing brakes wherever she drove from other drivers who were annoyed or trying not to hit her. Yet it wasn't until late in life that she had an accident.

"I've never had an accident," she would say. "I'm a good driver."

"Never had one, maybe," I conceded, "but you caused 'em. You've been very lucky."

She would frown. "You guys are always picking on my driving."

As a youngster in the sixties, with the exception of very short trips, I always vomited when she was driving. This enraged her, and she would gun the gas in frustration to get me home or to wherever we were going to recover. This scared the crap out of me because she never reached even the speed limit and now she was exceeding it, and she didn't manage speed well. It was a nightmare, her swerving all over the road with squealing tires, adding emotional discomfort to my physical.

"Just stop it. This is psychosomatic; it's all in your head. Don't you get enough attention?"

I didn't know how to "just stop it," and I got no direction. I grew to dread being in the car with my mother behind the wheel. I had discovered that sleeping or at least resting with my head back and my eyes closed kept sickness at bay. But my industrious mother, ever the busy one, made use of all her waking hours to be productive. She would reach a light and pump the brakes to bounce my head and keep me alert.

"Sleeping is a waste of your life," she'd say. "You can sleep when you're dead."

She wanted me to do homework under her tutelage, or read, to use the car time wisely. This was a special kind of torture for me and always resulted in vomit, then anger and speed, then home and sweet relief. My stomach roiling with bile, my head spinning and disoriented, the sweat, then the clammy threat of vomit. Though I was unable to express much other than my discomfort, my annoyance internalized with her implication of my laziness and lack of drive. An avid reader, I would have loved nothing more than to read in the car. Many was the night I spent under my covers with my Girl Scout flashlight, reading. Fortunately for me, my more confident dad drove when we were all together. I still couldn't read when he drove, motion sickness being a real thing, and not my fake attempt to avoid work. As soon as I got my license, I was her passenger only rarely.

Long before she was a captive in memory care, my mother's driving skills deteriorated significantly. She became more and more anxious, and she began driving in the center of the road or to the left. Her husband shrugged his shoulders when it was mentioned to him. "What do you want me to do? She has to drive herself places." She was a danger to herself and others, so we sought help from the police. They suggested we bring her to

DMV and have her tested. We tried talking to her about this. She stomped her feet and walked away, yelling as she disappeared, telling us in no uncertain terms we would not be stealing her independence from her.[1]

"No one is taking my keys from me!"

We tried her doctor, who was clueless. "Your mother is a lovely woman; she's just a little forgetful at times."

"But she drives left."

"Then just offer to drive her. I'm sure she'll comply."

Yeah, thanks for that. My mother was such a compliant sort. Help finally came from the creativity of my husband, Brodie, and our mechanic, Joe. Brodie realized she had become quite literal in her speech and understanding. This is an insight that gets lost, I think, when you're the relative on the front line caring for someone. You have a set of expectations for their competence, which have been established over a lifetime. When she said "no one is taking my keys from me" she meant just that. Keys represented freedom to her. She had not thought further.

We came to realize she had reached a point where, if her car did not start, she wouldn't be able to problem-solve her way out of it. We weren't even sure she knew what to do with the keys once she got in the car. She wouldn't have ever opened the hood to see what was going on if it didn't start. She never did anything of the sort. That was Joe's task. If the car didn't start, she would most likely call him at the corner gas station a few miles from her house.

Brodie took out the battery and left a note in the cavity to whomever might crack the hood that the driver had dementia and to contact Joe at a corner station a few miles down the road apiece. For Joe's part, he assured us he had done the very same

---

1. Driving requires attention, judgement, memory, visuospatial skills, and motor coordination. Alzheimer's disease progressively impairs these abilities, increasing crash risk over time. National Institute on Aging. "Driving Safety and Alzheimer's Disease." Updated 2023. https://www.nia.nih.gov/health/safety/driving-safety-and-alzheimers-disease.

thing for many families. I guess we weren't alone. So if she ever made it down the plan so far as Joe getting called, he would tow the car to the station, and she would be told he was ordering a part—indefinitely. She had no concept of time anymore. Her keys would stay in the key drawer in her kitchen, and she would be none the wiser.

While it was a wonderful and gentle solution to a significant problem, it left me bereft. It was loaded with loss and grief as I had gained a deeper understanding of her deficits, and the degree to which she was disappearing in front of our eyes.

Answering Machine

"Hi, you must not be home. I bet you're out grocery shopping, or maybe I forgot and you have class today . . . I suppose you might have stayed late at work, or maybe you're out with one of your friends, having a good time . . . I hope you're having a good time . . . If you can, would you please call me at your earliest inconvenience? I have some mail here for you at the house that says 'Open Immediately' and I don't want there to be a delay in you getting something important . . . Well okay, I hope you call me back soon. Call me back, okay? This is Mommy."

It's the late eighties, I'm a grown adult, and this is a short example of the messages my mother would leave on my answering machine. This is a time before the ubiquitous nature of cell phones. Her messages, replete with pauses; her anxiety about junk mail that still came to her house for me after over ten years of not living there; and the inevitable sign-off. As though I would not know it was her, she used a moniker I'd not used since my primary school days. The messages always speculated on why I wasn't answering the phone and always expressed some immediate need requiring my attention. These happened while my father was alive, too, but to a much lesser extent. After he died, they became urgent and lonely. She would leave a dozen or more in rapid succession, so by the time I got home at the end of a full day of teaching and then grad school, I would have no fewer than six, and often up to twenty messages from her, depending on her level of anxiety or loneliness at the time. She left the pauses in her messages, I think, because she was under the impression that if she left just the right grabber, I'd pick up the phone (because I must be sitting right next to it) and talk to her. I did not ignore my mother's phone calls, but it got to the point where I wanted to.

"I know I just called, but I thought I might catch you coming in the door . . . Are you coming in? Did I catch you? Can you hear me? . . . Call me, I have something to tell you. You must be at class, or maybe you're studying, but I wish you would pick up the phone . . . I have important things to share with you that I think you will want to hear . . . I will be in the shop but I will have the phone with me so I can answer right away when you call . . . Okay? . . . Okay, I'll talk to you soon. Don't forget to call me . . . It's Mommy, by the way."

It became a chore to collect the messages at the end of the day. If I did not respond with relative haste, she would either call me late at night while I slept—"Oh! Did I wake you? I thought you'd be up" (because, of course, you can sleep when you're dead)—or come across town and bang on my door to see if I were okay. There was no escaping my mother if she wanted to talk to me. Listening to her prattle on and on in the messages became a frustration and then an exercise in patience.

I ran with it, having compassion for her loneliness after thirty-five years of marriage. It was loneliness to which I chalked up the behavior. She felt deserted every time she was unable to reach me and assumed I was avoiding her. Even if I were home and answered the phone, she was likely to call a half dozen times in one evening. "Did I remember to tell you I have mail for you here? You should come pick it up. It says it's important."

Looking back, it was part of the beginning. It was surely in response to the loss of my dad, but the insidiousness of Alzheimer's is that it inserts itself into familiar behaviors and exacerbates them. The trauma my mother experienced at the loss of her husband became not only an augmentation of her anxieties but a catalyst for a further foothold of the disease.

Thanksgiving of the Chocolate Cream Pie

Thanksgivings had been held at my family home until the year after my dad died. My mother was an inept cook, and my dad always good-naturedly complained about the work and the snitching (this was how he referred to stealing food when he wasn't looking, which my mother and I took great delight in, then tried to look all innocent with our mouths full when he caught us) as he cooked, served, and basked in praise for what was always a wonderful meal. My mother attended to polishing silver, perfecting place settings, and arranging flowers, always flowers, with bobeches in the candelabra and the centerpiece. It was a perfect marriage of skill. My dad was a terrific cook, and my mother was the welcoming hostess. My mother didn't cook except for one "traditional" dessert. She loved not having to cook.

The year he died, we attempted to do up a regular Thanksgiving and largely succeeded despite the empty chair. I had studied at his elbow in the kitchen over the years, asked a billion questions, and as I grew older, became his sous-chef. This year, we had my mom make her signature dessert beforehand, and we sliced and diced and prepared while she chatted us up in the kitchen. The table was set, silver polished to a fine patina, heirloom napkin rings in their right places, and the autumn flowers as beautiful as ever. The chair was empty at the head. We felt the absence but were well determined to be cheerful and thankful. When it came time to carve the turkey, my mom handed me the knife. I handed it back to her and said, "I don't *know* how to carve a turkey." She looked at me astonished and said, "*I* don't know how to carve a turkey." Turning to my fiancé I handed him the knife and asked, "Can you please carve the turkey?" His now predictable response was "I don't know *how* to carve a turkey."

We hacked the turkey in this pre-Google time, through tears and chuckles, recognizing the absurdity and feeling the loss. We ate dinner without further ado and even enjoyed some games. Later we chuckled a bit more sans tears at our carving debacle. It was only months later we were able to give it a hearty laugh. But Thanksgiving that year was flat and empty and forever changed. My mother said maybe she would give it up. Christmas was her focus, so I took the reins on Thanksgiving traditions.

By the time she was incarcerated in the memory unit, the traditions had been augmented, and the level of expectation for the day was high for fun and familiarity, and a bit of raucousness. Once we had taken over the holiday, she came to love what we did with the day, honoring her traditions, and the band of regulars and transients who were welcomed each year, many at her behest. She always looked forward to it and always made her dessert: Indian pudding, which no one ate but her and me. The recipe came out of her white *Woman's Home Companion* (1942: P.F. Collier and Son Corp.) cookbook. It's an acquired taste, or one that you grow up with and associate with a holiday. Made with corn meal, molasses, and a variety of spices, it was a dark brown custard, from a cookbook whose editors thought nothing of perpetuating the derogatory name it acquired from the New England settlers' name for cornmeal: Indian meal.

We held dinner late so that friends who had family obligations during the day might join us for the evening. We moved out all our furniture, and the table took up our whole living room. It was elbow-to-elbow seating, though there was always room for Elijah. Traditions were added each year by us and our guests, and by now they included the question "Who knows how to carve a turkey?" when the bird came out of the oven.

Part of the insidiousness of Alzheimer's is the stealthy way in which it seems to begin by augmenting our eccentricities. My mother was not accomplished in the kitchen, and stories abound of her escapades therein. She dried flowers on low heat in her oven for projects she was completing but forgot they were there and preheated the oven for food, burning them and sending smells of scorched detritus throughout the house. So calamitous and messy were her interactions with the kitchen, we joked that the cabinets burst open and the canisters spilled in greeting even if she were just walking through. She continued to make the pudding, but each year it got worse and worse—even for those of us who liked it. Not only did she forget ingredients, but she also forgot to turn on the oven, or forgot it was cooking in the oven, or how to bake it, or how to follow the directions. There was always some reason she gave why it wasn't just right. Looking back, these were signs of increasing concern, but my mother was such a poor cook and so scattered so much of the time with all her multitasking, that to be honest, it surprised no one and provoked no worry.

That last Thanksgiving before her incarceration, she was at our table sans pudding. She didn't remember that she used to make it or that it was a staple at that point. I made her favorite pie for the first time at that meal, knowing I'd be able to get her to eat it. She wasn't eating much those days. She forgot what she was doing after each mouthful, and then said she was full when coaxed. Pies at Thanksgiving were traditionally from the harvest —apple, pumpkin, pecan, and the like—but that year I added chocolate cream pie (her favorite) to the menu.

Even though we don't seat family members next to one another at our Thanksgiving table, that year I sat next to her to shepherd her through the meal because she was becoming increasingly befuddled. She was happy to see old friends and to be social, and she seemed to enjoy the bustle and chatter, though she was decidedly quiet. When it was time for dessert, I put the pie right in front of her and told her I had made it just for her. "You *did*?!" As though no one had ever done such a thing for her in her life. I ceremoniously cut her the first slice and showed her where her dessert fork was, something she'd have been appalled to know she had forgotten. She commented several times about how good it was and finished every last crumb. My mother was never one to refuse a piece of chocolate cream pie. I enjoyed watching her work her way through it as much as she enjoyed eating it, despite the thought tugging at my brain about how much she was withering away. I offered her another piece, knowing she would decline in order to keep her girlish figure (but sneak more later). I would send the rest home with her, and she would eat it for breakfast every day till it was gone. Pie for breakfast was her favorite post-Thanksgiving tradition.

I was halfway through my pumpkin pie when I got a tap on the wrist and a little voice asked, "May I"—always *may* I—"have a piece of the chocolate pie? It's my favorite."

"Sure, Mom, I didn't know you wanted another; I'm glad you said something."

"I haven't had *any* yet," said she. Of course she got another piece, and I loved watching her enjoy it again for the first time. I held back the tears for both the lack of memory, and that she thought I'd not offered her a piece to begin with. She could've eaten the whole pie for all I cared. We talked about chocolate cream pie while she ate it. If she were going to live in the moment, then I was going to make sure those moments were as rich as possible. She refused the next piece that was offered with, "Maybe I'll have some with dessert."

December

One Lonely Gift

The phone rings and vibrates as I've set it to do. *Can't miss a call.* Adrenaline rushes, heart races, palms and neck sweat, face flushes in those fractions of reactive time before my brain signals my hand to reach. It could be my husband, my roomie from college, my girls, or another dear friend. But at this point, calls were beginning to come from the memory unit as often as the calls had come from the creep when my mother was still home. Always a breathless crisis. Then, he would request I use my influence to "get her" to watch a movie or Fox News that squawked urgently all day in the background, so he didn't have to engage with her. This was his only solution to helping her. My suggestions for things he might do fell on deaf ears. Perhaps they were overwhelming. He eschewed help, and she continued her decline.

I don't remember my mother ever sitting still to watch anything on TV. She was always in and out of the room, doing one thing or another and then returning and asking what had happened while she was gone. It was pretty annoying. Now she was wandering and casting about randomly for attention, interaction, companionship. I'm vexed; he can't be bothered. When I hear his voice complaining about these things, I feel like a cat ready to strike—the hair on the back of my neck stands up and tingles, and I can almost feel a tail, whipping big and threatening. I felt he wanted a quiet housemate who would provide intimate and financial benefits but otherwise allow for an unfettered, unemployed leisure life of freedom, which could remain unchanged by the disease. Me? Influence her? HA!! Like I'd ever been able to do that.

I had expected the memory unit placement would provide a reprieve from expectations that *I* would manage her behaviors day in and day out. I also expected these professionals would engage her, include her, help her feel connected. Now I was getting calls regularly to inform me that my mother was being, well, herself. Who the fuck did you expect her to be? My mother was and always had been her own woman. Smart, intellectual, independent. A bit oppositional, she was likely to do the exact opposite of what was requested just for the sake of it. She wanted to talk about flowers and the seasons, so she knocked on doors. She wanted to talk about professional things and imaginary clients, so she sought out the nurses when the residents who sat on the couch watching TV gave her blank stares. She wanted to go to work or meet a friend for lunch. She likely would have been grateful for the spaces designed for wandering were she able to think about it: She had been confined to two rooms at home for months now so he could keep track of her and still maintain his reclusive life of myriad old coffee cups cluttered around his monitors and gaming equipment where he spent his days hunched over and talking to himself, gaming, and jumping down internet rabbit holes.

The complaints continued. By this time, the phone-call-dread was in constant hover. Always something that seemed inconsequential. What now?

"Your mother won't allow an aide to assist her in the shower."

"Does she get herself clean?"

"Well, yes, but we like to make sure."

"Does she smell?"

"Well, no, but she could get infections."

"Does she have an infection?"

"No, she does not, but we'd like to keep it that way."

Her clothes didn't match. She wore too many shirts. She always wanted to talk. She wouldn't watch TV. She kept asking when my dad would come to pick her up. *Who cares?* She wanted to chat up the nurses and they had work to do. *Um, wait, wasn't she their work?* I truly didn't understand. I thought she should be allowed whatever privacy was not detrimental to her, that staff would facilitate engagement as promised, and unless something was harmful, she'd be allowed to do it no matter how perseverative. This was the nature of the disease. It seemed to me they wanted a very specific docile personality in their facility that my mother did not have and never had. What were all the interviews for if they had not assessed who she was and how she was likely to fit? Each time the call came, the heat of anxiety and frustration rose that much faster in my chest and it never stopped festering in between calls. I was in low-level fight mode all the time now. Where would she possibly go if they couldn't manage her there? Why couldn't they manage her there? We'd been managing her for months. They said she needed to be there for safety.

After a few weeks in residence, they requested my mother have an appointment with their consulting psychiatrist for a medication evaluation to see if they could make her days "less agitated" and her nights more peaceful for the staff while she slept rather than soldiering around. They wanted to medicate her into compliance. I agreed, but with resentment and anger. I was snappish and borderline rude; I felt out of control, at sixes and sevens, with no way to control my mother, no way to assuage my fears for my mother, and disappointed in myself for not being able to help my mother. This weighed heavy on my mind. Had they no strategies for helping an old, confused woman feel included?

The meds they prescribed did not work quickly enough to appease the staff. They had no patience for her. These medications sometimes took months to reach a therapeutic effect. What the fuck? They should have known that. Subsequent calls came with gauzy threats that her behavior would have to change if they were going to keep her. Now the calls brought a full-on adrenaline rush, the heat beginning in my head and stinging its way down my spine before I even picked up the phone.

On my last day of work before Christmas break, I had comforting and even relaxing thoughts of no phone calls, since she would be home with me within hours for a visit. That morning there was a gentle Advent snow when I woke. It was also our wedding anniversary, three days before Christmas. I stole a few moments for myself, taking my morning tea to the back porch in my bare feet to feel the cold and listen to the snow fall before I left for work, like my mother and I had done in the dark of a snowfall in years gone by. I allowed myself some joy in anticipation of her visit, the holiday preparations, and a full family table. "Shield the joyous," says *The Book of Common Prayer*.

Before I knew it, I was at midmorning in a packed day. By this time tomorrow, I would be on break, and she would be home with us. The days before a holiday break often bring anxieties and crises. The children who want to go on break can be excited beyond control, and the ones who don't want to go on break sometimes act out as they struggle with the transition. I was in the throes of the day and even so, by this time, the background phone-call-dread was still a hovering constant companion.

The damn phone rang. *What now? All these rushing thoughts.* I picked up on the third ring: "Hello?" Impending doom filled my chest, heavy and thick this time with heat and pressure. *The interruption. The exasperation. The annoyance. The worry. The guilt. Another Damn Call.* I felt the adrenaline-dread and realized that nothing had changed from when my mother had been home. Still folks calling to say they don't know what to do with her. Still looking to me for influence and answers. Still, always, the guilt that I couldn't fix it. I was tempted not to answer. *They can do their damn job while I do mine; I'll be there to get her in a few hours.*

"Hello?" The heartbeat of space before a response, three days before a family Christmas, her first visit back with us, just two months after her admittance, and inside the window that I had been told was part of the adjustment period. *THIS IS PART OF THE ADJUSTMENT PERIOD!! WHAT THE FUCKING FUCK?! I'M PICKING HER UP ONLY HOURS FROM NOW. WHAT COULD YOU POSSIBLY NEED FROM ME?*

"Your mother went out into the gardens this morning in the snow in her bare feet and pajamas."

"Yes, she enjoys listening to and watching the snowfall."

"This is not acceptable behavior, and she refused redirection, making threats to escape."

Escape? It really was incarceration.

This sojourn into the gardens was no surprise to me. I'd done it that very morning. The memory facility had beautiful gardens that flowered around the seasons and were accessible to the residents. The paths meandered and looped, always leading back to safety. The entire unit was a maze like this, with only one locked entry point to the outside. This was the door I used to come and go freely. When they encouraged her to go back into the building, they claimed that she refused and ran, saying, "I'm gonna climb those walls right there and get out!" Liars—my mother *never* ran, because "a lady doesn't run."

This "threat" from my 4'11", ninety-five-pound mother against a smooth ten-foot wall was the prompt for a trip in an ambulance to the Community Home Alzheimer's psych unit across town. She had been strapped down, dispatched, and delivered before they called me to say she was "a danger to self and others" on the memory unit.

In my adolescence, when my mother's and my relationship was the most tempestuous, one or the other of us would pull each other like warm taffy from bed in the middle of the night in complete silence. We would pad out to the flagstone porch or straight into the yard, hands clasped, to listen to snowfall or stand in awe of a full moon rendering my mother's Kodachrome gardens an enchanted silver forest. This was done in silence, and it was never spoken of in daylight hours. It was a mutual joy that just happened. Sobs caught in my throat thinking of her lonely attempt to recreate this only to be yanked into the harshness of rules and policies.

They matter-of-factly informed me they had made me an appointment with a psychiatrist on the unit for that afternoon to discuss her evaluation. No question if I could make it, just the expectation that I would drop everything because my mother wanted to walk the snowy garden in her bare feet and got angry when someone told her she couldn't. I hurriedly rearranged my work schedule and raced to my car. I don't remember the drive in snow.

There was no pretense at the Community Home. The unit was in the oldest part of the building and looked frozen in time. Stark, unapologetic, functional. My mother had been placed in an Alzheimer's Psychiatric Unit. *Ward.* It looked for all the world like a hospital from the 1950s: drab, spartan, undecorated, dirty old beige. The walls and floors were cracked, faded, chipped ceramic and linoleum tiles respectively, with missing pieces and black grout from years of use and God knows what other stains. I expected to see nurses with caps starched to within an inch of their lives, white stockings, and white uniforms with school pins like my grandmother had worn when she was working. I was to meet the psychiatrist on the unit. A locked unit. *She'd been locked up since before this began. Escape. Incarceration.*

The doors had safety windows with wire mesh in the glass and circles of condensation where imprisoned folks had pressed noses against them to get glimpses of the world outside. Some residents stood a few feet back, hoping to go unnoticed and sneak out when doors were opened. When I buzzed in, a nurse came down the hall from the nurse's station—a cage really, with the same meshed windows and a panoramic view where she sat isolated from the ward's population. Her arms were swinging in all directions, gesticulating as she barked at the residents. The small sea of folks parted as she came through, and they scurried silently away as the doors opened. The thud that echoed in my head as the doors closed behind me was only a click, but it evoked a prison door like I'd heard in movies. My world and sense of time shifted.

Stale urine, old lady breath, and desperation hit me full force. As directed, I waited by the nurses' station for the psychiatrist, who was almost as old and crusty as those he was serving. He all but shuffled to me, walking slowly, hunched over and intent as though carrying a great weight he could not shift for fear of dropping it. His back was bent forward so his profile was almost parallel to the floor and he had to peer up through stringy white hair to make eye contact, which he did fleetingly. He smelled of sweat and exhaustion. His white shirt, once pressed, was wrinkled as though he had slept in it, and had yellow stains at the armpits. His accompanying tie with a full Windsor looked as though it had been knotted a decade before and slipped on and off over his head since then when the situation called for it. The wool vest he wore was misshapen, shorter on one side than the other, missing a mid-belly braided leather button, the original color some shade of dull.

He responded, "Mmmm" when I introduced myself, and indicated the direction to his office—not an office at all but a supply closet where he'd managed to squirrel away a computer. There, amongst the metal shelves of towels and sheets, and masks and pee pads, he asked a few basic medical history questions about my mother. He dismissed my descriptions of her personhood, her likes and dislikes, or her needs and desires. As he scratched cryptic medi-speak on her chart, he reported in an automatic monotone that she would be well cared for, and her behavior would be managed.

"Your mother is difficult," he pronounced, going on to imply that if she were medicated into submission just short of drooling, perhaps she could return to her original placement. "It will take several weeks"—but Countryside Care expected immediate change—"for us to determine her response," he continued. "No,

I'm sorry, she cannot be released for Christmas. You'll have to ask the nurses where she is; I haven't met her."

He hasn't even met her? Wait! No Christmas? My mother had become a chart, a file, a less-than-interesting, non-unique number that required a series of protocols be applied. He left the closet, shuffling and grunting past my stunned self.

I gulped for air, unaware I'd been holding my breath. Mechanically, I took up my hunt for the ever-so-difficult woman. In the iconic Day Room at the arts-and-crafts table with a pile of snarled dirty yellow yarn in her lap, she was waving an empty knitting needle *(in the psych unit?!)* as though it were a conductor's baton (still leading her own score), attempting to knit, a skill she had never learned. She was content in what she was doing, and not the least bit agitated. *For the love of God, she's not yet been medicated.*

I sat with her awhile. She was happy to see me and chatted away in a nonsense of verbs and nouns in their correct grammatical places having no theme or continuity, her own personal word salad Mad Lib without the humor. When I left, she picked up again with her symphony. The cage nurse scattered the residents again and buzzed me out. I headed home to the empty chair on Christmas Day. One gift under the tree would never be given, opened, or needed.

Taking It All Away

Our family attorney, born the same year as my mother and of sound mind, was reluctant to help in affording me legal control over her life, even though her husband (whose finances were completely separate, partly by the lawyer's design) was suspected of abusing her by the admitting memory facility. There was no proof and no investigation. She was writing him checks off her home equity account after being badgered each time for days to do so, and her unpaid bills were resulting in cancellations and shutoffs. She allowed no assistance with this from me or anyone else, including her attorney, insisting she was on it.

When my mother was first placed in a memory care facility, the legal aspect of it was all very gray. They assured me she was safer there than at home because they suspected the creepy husband was abusing her, though they conducted no investigation, did not contact the town social worker or protective services, and provided no proof. I did not doubt the improved safety regardless of concerns about abuse (with so many eyes around, structure to her day, and medication administration, which he had left her to do on her own), though placement seemed legally precarious and only marginally more dignified.

Not being able to sleep and having no one to chat up (because staff had work to do and told her to go back to bed), she had committed no crime except entering the beautiful gardens she so loved in her bare feet and pajamas just before sunrise to watch the snow fall. Something we had done together so many times while I was growing up it would be near impossible to count. When she "ran" from two security folks who had been sent to fetch her, they "carried" her inside where her protestations grew louder and angrier, and her arms flailed in distress. It was then they made the call to the other home.

Now, strapped to a gurney, potentially in a straitjacket (though I would never know as she would not recall, or would be ashamed to say, and they wouldn't tell), my mother was whisked off across town to the psych unit of another larger eldercare facility. This was the day I was to pick her up to come home with us for Christmas. I was not called by her memory care facility or this new facility until late into the morning.

In another time, my mother worked tirelessly to maintain my grandmother's autonomy and independence—long past the time she should have done. Even though I watched this through my high school and college years and became frustrated for my grandmother, who required round-the-clock care long before she got it, my mother's multiple daily ministrations to my grandmother became the road map for me. No matter what I said to my mother, she insisted my grandmother had earned and deserved her independence. *Follow the roadmap; don't take it all away unless you absolutely must.*

The assault on my mother's dignity, autonomy, and independence came too late, just as it had for her mother before her, when she was removed from memory care by force to the Alzheimer's psych unit. There, they were a well-oiled legal machine, with dotted i's and crossed t's. When I had previously reached out to everyone for help with my mother, from the town social worker to her doctor, and even to her church, I ran into outright refusals. But the psych unit knew what to do and how to do it.

Within a few hours of her arrival, I was summoned to meet with the psychiatrist, and not twenty-four hours later they had made an appointment to attend to the issue of her competence. There is only so much time on a psych hold, and they had a plan to expedite her new care program.

"Yes, I can be there at ten tomorrow. Will I need paperwork?"

"No, ma'am. We have everything you'll need right here. We need to take care of this within forty-eight hours."

I was stunned. "Really?"

"Yes, ma'am. The courtroom is on the second floor, room 210. We will see you then."

The courtroom? The new home was a little city. It had everything: different dining halls with different cuisines, salon, barbershop, bank, boutique, spa with manicurist, hospital, gym, pool, coffee shop, gardens, jitney to take you places, library, ice cream shop, anything you could imagine. Including a courtroom. With a judge.

No part of this new wonderful eldercare facility would be accessible to my mother, because she was confined to a locked psych unit.

I arrived in the parking lot on the appointed morning with fifteen minutes to spare. I did not know the entrance to this section of the building as it was not the main one. It was off to the side. No effort had been taken to make it inviting like the landscaped front entrance with pleasing architectural details and beautiful plantings. It was austere, bare.

Mumbling to myself, I walked along a barely cleared sidewalk, swearing because I'd not worn sturdier winter shoes to keep my feet warm and dry. Slush was not as fun to walk in as snow. Once inside I put one foot in front of the other to the elevators and down the hallways of the business end of the facility. I could not focus on what I might need to say or defend. I could not put two cohesive thoughts together. Instead, memories and explanations fought for attention, ricocheting around my cranium like balls in a bingo cage. The halls were cold, though the heat was on in corridors with lined cinder block walls thickly painted and sometimes chipped. Long fluorescent lights hummed from the ceiling, adding a deceitful chemical brightness to the windowlessness. Functional large institutional linoleum squares covered the floors, some sections patched with newer cleaner squares, still gray, though they may have been some other muted color at one time. The décor was completed with brown rubber mopboard.

My footsteps echoed and bounced in the empty halls much like my thoughts, passing the windows of one tiny dark office after another. They had names like "Maintenance," "Entertainment," "Recreation," "Visiting Nurses," "Podiatrist." Desolate and totally uninviting, this was not what the residents or prospective residents saw. These were the bowels of the industry.

Already emotionally exhausted, I found 210. "Courtroom" was painted on the blurry shower-glass windowed door. Hesitant, I pushed it open and poked my head around. I was encouraged to enter by an emphatic gesture from the only other person there. An old geezer, easily ten years my mother's senior. It took me a beat to register him as the judge. He had cuff

links on his blue-white monogrammed oxford, and his clothes were pressed to the hilt, though not much could be done for his wrinkled face. His chins flowed into his neck from his gauntness, giving the impression that he had no jawbone.

The room did not feel solid or imposing the way one would expect from a court. No columns, no bench. No statue of Justice, blindfolded, holding balanced scales. The only one blinded here was my mother, and the scales were not balanced. Instead, there were folding chairs and a large folding table that squeaked; there were no special chairs or robes, even for the judge. It all gave the appearance it could be disassembled right quick in the dark of the night, and the name on the door replaced with "Machine Room."

His voice was authoritative, though.

"All right, let's get this taken care of. We will conserve your mother today. The staff psychiatrist, in his professional opinion, has deemed she is not able to tend to her own affairs. He's spoken to you, hmm? Sign here."

I did so mechanically. Was *I* able to attend to my own or her affairs?

"Good girl. One more place"—as he shuffled papers—"mm-hmm, right there."

"Do you need paperwork?" I wondered. "Her will? Health-care proxy? Power of attorney?"

"No, we have everything you need right here"—he tapped the documents with his index finger—"and you've just completed it." Rising from his protesting chair, he beckoned the next head to poke around the door. "Come on in."

Five minutes.

A planned, scheduled, five minutes of efficiency I'd been heretofore unable to access, to reduce my mother to little more than a child and strip her of the last vestiges of hope for some measure of autonomy or independence.

I don't remember getting back down the hall, down the elevator, out the not-main entrance, into the slush to my car, or driving back to work.

Urgent Stern Stars on a Crystal Velvet Landscape

Evening of a frosty grey day
warm flannel nightgown
tucked into a good book, cat warming my lap.
Early flakes plink insistently outside on the window.
Uncurl and stretch with the kitty—
Slow luxury.

Bare feet pound and press porch flagstone.
Cold barely registering over flakes swirling,
Falling
Crunching
Interlocking.
Streetlights glow like distant candles,
hazy summer flaxen against the greywhite.

Day will blink and blind brighter than the beach in high summer.
Then a new evening
Lazy opaque crescent moonbowl.
Cold.
Clear.
Crisp.

One Missing Chair

When I was young, the dinner table was a lonely place, but especially lonely on the holidays when all my friends were talking about siblings and cousins and out-of-town relatives crowded around tables shoved together, or the hijinks at the children's table. My family of five all fit at the dining room table—it didn't occur to anyone to take away the extra empty chairs. Me, my parents, and my maternal grandparents, with what felt like the Great Plains between each of us. It wasn't that we didn't have cousins and friends and out-of-town relatives—we just didn't see much of them, and we certainly didn't spend the holidays with them. It was never well explained why we didn't consort with the family. Fissures were hinted at but never clarified, and when I asked, I was told curtly it wasn't my business. My cousins and I wonder about it now but still don't know.

Our holidays traditionally lacked attendees, but were full of traditions, and these I looked forward to with great anticipation and excitement. The table setting, the holiday dishes, my dad's cooking, the Christmas cookies with my mother. The decorations that began in fall and changed monthly in increasing volume until the great crescendo from Advent into Christmas.

There were rules about Christmas carols: never before midnight on Thanksgiving. I was finally allowed to stay up until midnight—a delicious win over bedtime for an eight-year-old. Over the years, I managed to whittle my mother down to sundown, then to just after dessert. It took years to get past dessert, though. The tree didn't go up until Christmas Eve, when the color of the house decorations changed from purples, lavenders, greens, and silvers to reds, greens, and golds.

My dad was a gifted artist who was a printer by trade. Every year he designed and silk-screened Christmas cards. Dad taught me to silk-screen when I was ten. To me he was larger than life, though not quite six feet tall and a bit rotund. He had wavy brown hair and deep brown eyes with a black dot in one iris. He designed and printed Christmas cards from the time my parents were first married. His cards were so beautiful there were folks who kept collections of them and put them out with their own decorations from year to year. I did a two-color tree my first time, a jaunty little silhouette of an evergreen with a yellow star atop. I loved the *wheeesh* of the squeegee on the silk and the rhythm of our walking back and forth as we helped each other lay out our cards to dry. I loved the smell of ink, green stencil, and the benzene. Oh, that benzene—in it up to my elbows. I loved this very special time with my dad, and later, when the cards were done, my mom and I would sit at the kitchen table and write notes and addresses on our cards for mailing. Then Mailing Day, also a ritual. The third Sunday of Advent. Marian Sunday. The pink candle on the Advent wreath.

Mom ritualized the unpacking and packing of decorations and ornaments, such that I looked forward to careful excavation of packing paper and wrapping to uncover treasures, each of which came with a story. "Auntie Lucia gave you that one for your first Christmas, and the blue one there is from Holland. Uncle Mark was there—it's very old—but Delft is still painted like that." By the time I was seven or so, I could tell most of the stories myself, and of course, to new things that got added I attached some of my own stories. Though my mother couldn't cook to save her soul, she could and did bake cookies. She made me part of this ritual also—and those times were full of flour dusting and gooey fingers and gingerbread men who always seemed to disappear before they were decorated. Those darn gingerbread men ran away! She never left the kitchen, and to this day I don't know how she made them disappear and reappear in other places in the house. One of my Christmas mysteries. While it was a lonely time, it was also a busy time, rich in story and ritual and music which I looked forward to with great anticipation. There wasn't much that changed about those traditions for a very long time.

My children have grown up with a very full table and many traditions, small and grand, that have expanded over the years, building a crescendo through the season. I passed on my holiday season traditions to them, and they still look forward to the old rituals practiced at my mother's home, inclusive of the new one: My mother switched from gingerbread men to gingerbread houses.

Then came the year of the fifteen-year-old daughter. It was Christmas Eve, and my mother had died the previous spring. My husband and two girls were in the process of decorating the tree and talking about the ornaments and their stories, the girls in Christmas velvet and ribboned hair, Brodie in his traditional Christmas plaid vest and bow tie. I left as things were wrapping up to shower and get ready for the evening meal and the later choir rehearsal before midnight service. I heard an argument erupt downstairs and came out to see what was brewing. My eldest flew past me on the way to her cave, and I made the mistake of asking what was wrong. "I hate Christmas, and I have for years!" she growled in the surliest sneer one could possibly imagine.

In that instant, and for many years after, I nursed a primordial hurt from those words, wondering where I had gone wrong and how I had made the holidays fraught with the angst so many describe, all while trying to fill them with the best the season has to offer. I strove to understand the invective and derision that had been communicated to me in those moments. I felt eviscerated and humiliated and hurt to the bone, all this time thinking my children had enjoyed what I worked so hard to maintain and had escaped the dread and jadedness with which so many approach the holidays.

The following year, I toned down the traditions, and the beast was quiet but clearly unhappy. She refused to discuss it. For each successive year, I dropped more and more. She got quieter and quieter, until I dropped the majority, thinking that somehow I could erase those moments and the pain that I had apparently unwittingly inflicted upon my daughter.

It wasn't until her freshman year at college that she sent me an email asking me to reinstate tradition around our holiday with an admonishment that we couldn't discuss it. It was just to be done. The email was accompanied by an essay she had written for a freshman class. In the essay, she talked about the richness and enjoyment of the holiday seasons she had experienced, and how acutely she felt the loneliness of the missing chair at the dinner table and the box with the Christmas gift that would never be given. We didn't talk about it. I just followed her lead and somehow, tenuously, the stories and rituals came back. I found The Gift under the tree on Christmas Eve, bedecked in one of my father's old wrapping papers, heavy, luxurious, and shiny, with a holly motif and a simple red bow encircling it. It had been tucked away behind the decorations in the attic. I couldn't part with it but didn't quite know what to do with it. I don't know who put it under the tree, but now it shows up there every year on Christmas Eve and disappears by Twelfth Night.

The-Blessed-Virgin-Mary-Mother-of-God

"Unconditional reverence" would describe the relationship my grandmother had with her own church. Everyone else was just wrong, of course, as it goes with Roman Catholics. She had a childlike faith layered with mysticism and lore I've only seen amongst Irish Catholics and those who honor the Kabbalah. She had a prescience many Irish would describe as fey, and she would say was indeed Fey in the form of the Holy Ghost. Her favorite prayer was: "Holy Ghost, enlighten me." She had prayers for everything. She prayed when she hung clothes on the line, when she ironed, when she cooked, when she baked bread, through her home days, her workdays, with patients she nursed in her Catholic hospital, with students with menstrual cramps at her school, and of course she prayed The Hours.

My grandmother, as she told it, never had sex again after my mother was born (her first and last). She was told it would kill her if she had another baby. The Church said sex was for procreation, and there would be no procreation. My mother had announced her presence with authority but refused the traditional entry, requiring a cesarean, but not before she ripped and tore things that should not have been ripped and torn. Or so the story goes. I could extrapolate fear of childbirth and loathing of a philandering husband as additional or more seminal reasons. But such is faith. We find in it what we need.

For as reverent as my grandmother was, my mother was irreverent. Wise in her own way, and a remarkably astute study of human foibles and failings, my mother had no prescience, preferring science and ascribing to skepticism when it came to her strictly adherent Roman Catholic upbringing. Her impish and resistant behavior began early. My grandmother said my mother was only in first grade when she snuck raisins under the back legs of the sheep and a prune behind the camel in the family heirloom crèche that went up with great ceremony on the first Sunday of Advent every year. She was admonished by my grandmother, which only encouraged her. They each reported she managed to sneak those dried fruits in their places for the remainder of her time in their home. Later, before the crèche came to live with us, Mom gave me raisins and a prune carefully wrapped in wax paper for my pockets when I was going to my grandmother's during Advent so I could carry on the tradition, giving me careful instructions about how to pile the raisins ... just*so*. I loved the story so much. It gave my mother a childlike aura hard to imagine in my younger years.

This irreverence continued through her high school years. Picture a statue in a Catholic all-girls high school of the Blessed-Virgin-Mary-Mother-of-God (said as one word by my grandmother and whispered as though a prayer) with her hand outstretched to the faithful. Blue dress, white mantle, bare feet on a religious orb of some sort. The Feast of the Immaculate Conception is in early December, and it is a Holy Day of Obligation, meaning you had to go to church even if it didn't fall on a Sunday. To miss an HDO was a mortal sin and would send you straight to hell, no questions asked.

In my mother's sophomore year, students all filed by the Blessed-Virgin-Mary-Mother-of-God on their way into chapel first thing on the morning of the Feast of the Immaculate

Conception to find an unlit cigarette between the fingers of Blessed-Virgin-Mary's hand and painted red toenails and finger-nails. My grandmother (who was the school nurse) and my mother's friends suspected who did it. No one told, she never admitted it, and she was never caught. Did she do it? I know not. I knew the story, though. She said her friends revisited it with varying detail on many of the occasions when they gathered through the years.

I think it no surprise my mother chose to marry a Protestant. My grandmother refused to meet him when he came to the door to pick up my mother for dates. She went to the basement to iron, leaving my grandfather to manage the encounter. In the time of their eventual union, it was a scandal to have a "mixed" marriage. My mother was oft quoted saying in her own brand of defiance that their marriage was not mixed as they were both Republicans. As it was, their first year of marriage was spent in an apartment just down the street from my grandparents, and my mother went to church with my grandmother (protecting her immortal soul from the fires of hell and the ire of my grandmother—the latter I suspect was worse), and my dad went off to his own heathen church. They would gather together afterward for one of my grandmother's famous brunches, replete with fresh or canned fruit salad (hers from when they were in season), warm croissants or French bread fresh out of the oven, her assortment of home-made jellies, and sliced candied ham to sweeten Sunday and break the fast.

One wonders if my mother's irreverence weren't baked into her, genetic, or visited upon her by the Fey. It came so naturally and often without forethought. Shortly after my parents were married and on one of my mother's breaks from school, my dad's rector made a house call to let her know she was welcome at church with my dad anytime (a sin in and of itself to darken the doorway of a Protestant church, never mind worship there) and to see if there were ways he could support the newlyweds. My mother had been industrious that morning. Among many chores and lesson plans, she was immersed in laundry and hanging clothing in available spaces around the apartment to dry (though I'm quite sure she didn't pray while doing so).

She graciously greeted the rector when he arrived, invited him in, and served him coffee and store-bought cookies on her new Lenox Wheat china, with linen napkins her favorite auntie had embroidered for her with her new last initial. They chatted amicably for the requisite and polite twenty minutes. After he left and she had cleaned up, my mother curled up with a good book in the wing chair in which the rector had been sitting. She looked up before she abandoned herself to the story she was reading and realized he had had a full view of the kitchen table while they were so agreeably chatting. On it was a too-large-for-the-table beautiful pair of perfectly polished sterling candelabra given as a wedding gift. To her horror, and then her absolute glee, she noted this was where she had conveniently hung her intimates to dry earlier that morning.

A Busy Wedding

Thirty-some-odd years ago, my mother planned a spectacular small wedding at her home for us in the weeks between Thanksgiving, when we had announced our engagement, and the twentieth of December, our wedding day. In her retirement, she had become a florist, and Christmas was her busiest time of year, but she took great enjoyment in making plans and discussing them with me.

She honored our wish for no more than thirty people, but otherwise we followed her lead. She pulled off a catered soup to nuts buffet on her own holiday dishes, with ironed and starched heirloom holiday linens, as well as elegant floral pieces of holly and white roses everywhere one could look. There was holly in the bobeches on the candelabra on the table, as well as graceful center-pieces and vases scattered throughout the house. No room was spared, and yet they all fit into the landscape as though they'd always been there. There was a tree in the foyer with just white lights, small silver and blue bows, and a single heart-shaped orna-ment with holly on it that had our names and the date. She did a piece for my hair and a small spray for her prayer book, which I held during the civil ceremony in lieu of a traditional bouquet, as well as requisite boutonnieres and corsages for mothers, fathers, and those standing up for us. We said our vows in the bend of her grand piano.

She spared no expense or detail—old (my grandmother's Irish lace handkerchief), new (flowers, undergarments), borrowed (the prayer book), blue (velvet wedding dress), an exquisite cake made by my godfather with my parents' top that I didn't even know she still had, and the knife my parents had used for their own wedding cake. I wore her pearl necklace, my grandmother's pearl bracelet, and my own pearl earrings.

The holiday dishes were of special significance. When she first married, my mother coveted the holiday dishes of her neighbors and friends who had been gifted or able to afford them. She had beautiful china, but nothing specific to the holidays. I began buying her single pieces of the pattern I knew she loved when I was about ten, for birthdays, Mother's Days, and Christmases, helping to build a set for our own small family holiday season. They were first used on Thanksgiving and got packed away at Epiphany (Twelfth Night—Three Kings) every year. By the time I got married she had more place settings for it than she did for her wedding pattern. It became a family joke that my mother could hold up her head among the other mothers in our highly accomplished community because she could take out the holiday dishes for her "daughter the doctor."

My mother thrived on the level of attention, detail, and energy required for all this wedding planning, alongside keeping up with her business and appearances. She had always thrived in chaos and demand—the more the better. A bit of an adrenaline junkie, she left things to the last minute but pulled it all together in the end. It meant many sleepless nights and fretful days. Were you to call her during these frenetic periods, she would answer the phone breathless, having just run from one place or the other to answer the wall phone in the kitchen, in a time before cordless phones and the omnipresent cell phone. When asked what she was doing that had her so breathless, she would respond, "I'm just so busy."

A mantra we knew well. Even when she would be sitting right next to the phone when it rang beside her library desk where she would be posted till the wee hours completing customers' bills in calligraphy with little messages for them because she insisted it was what they expected of her and what set her apart, she would still answer the phone breathless. She found ways to stay busy. Those bills on watermarked, chain-laid paper cut to a nonstandard size were small works of art. Works of love. They were never framed though, and likely ended up at the bottom of the circular file. "I'm just so busy." It killed me to think of the hours she spent on those damn bills, knowing that the customers read them, wrote their checks, and tossed them.

Her busy schedule kept her at a social distance from small talk, serving the same purpose as her garden. Small talk made her uncomfortable when she was around people. It cost her too. Just a few short years later she would miss opportunities to be with her grandchildren because of her schedule, to take out holiday decorations or dishes, or spend time with family and friends during the holiday season. There were, no doubt, losses she could not bear by then, my father having died the year before our wedding. We had a metaphorical brief glimpse on our wedding night, just after dinner, when everyone was looking for her so we could cut the cake. I have the photo of her in the foyer next to the tree put up just for us, standing in a gorgeous dress with a single white rose and a sprig of holly pinned on her breast, leaning against the wall, sound asleep.

January

Lunch

On this January day I join Mom for lunch. I have the day off, which I didn't expect her to remember. I find her in the dining room with her back ramrod straight against the sticky dining chair and her hands folded primly in her lap. She is talking to herself, fussing about her tray. At times she reaches up in front of her face and picks at something in the air.

"Whatcha doin', Mom?" I ask, pulling another sticky chair close to sit next to her.

"I'm getting all the strings, see 'em?"

Lunch is brisket, potato pancakes, applesauce, and green beans. Before my arrival, she'd asked one of the dining room attendants for sour cream and her napkin. There is a folded paper napkin on the tray to the left of her plate. Placement by Emily Post.

"I'll not use that! *I* use linen napkins and my napkin ring!"

It's going to be one of *those* visits.

There's nothing particularly classy about napkin rings. They don't belong at formal tables. Made from all kinds of materials, from wood, acrylic, and papier-mâché, to cut toilet paper rolls decorated with construction paper like my kids made when young, napkin rings were originally for the larger families or boarding houses, for people to mark their napkin as their own, as napkins were not washed after every meal. In our house we used cloth napkins so as not to waste paper (my dad was a printer) and to use up remnants from sewing. Few of our napkins matched, some were patched, and we used the rings as intended, changing them on our own when we felt the need. My mother had taken many a paper napkin graciously in stride as a guest in her friends' homes and in restaurants. Today she was being persnickety.

"And I want my sour cream," she says as she distractedly picks at the air.

"Whatcha doin', Mom?"

"You *asked* me that," she sneers. "I'm getting the strings, see 'em?"

"Well, let's get started while you wait, Ma."

I know full well that neither linen napkin nor napkin ring would come, nor were the strings likely to disappear unless meds were adjusted. Sour cream would not be provided either. The attendants had cheerfully acknowledged her request and moved on to the next resident. Normally, this tactic worked because she would forget, but today she is perseverating. Looking for ways to distract her, I grab one of the pancakes, dip it in applesauce, and munch away. It's crispy on the outside and soft on the inside. They've put a few carrots and beets in, probably leftovers, and it's sweeter than usual. Clever way to get veggies into the folks and not waste food.

"Mm-hmm, Ma, these are really good. Almost as good as mine."

"This! Is *peasant* food!" She spits out the words like a rotten mouthful. "And they can't even serve it with something sophisticated like sour cream. I. Don't. Like. *Peasant.* Food."

Who knew sour cream was the height of sophistication? My dad was famous for mean potato pancakes served with sauerbraten and red cabbage, which she requested he make regularly. Here though, they were apparently peasant food. I thought it was a reasonable midday meal for a population who ate like birds, and for whom the midday meal was likely the most consistently consumed. It smelled good, hit all the food groups, and was seasoned well, even if there were no linens.

"We need to go someplace better than this next time we go for lunch, dear. The waitress has given me no attention. I *still* don't have sour cream or my napkin ring."

She doesn't remember my name, but she knows she doesn't have her napkin ring or sour cream. The confabulation of monogrammed napkin rings at a restaurant is typical of her understanding these days. What isn't consistent is that I can't distract her. While her mood might be grouchy, I was often able to get her to jump from one grouch to another, just to spread the wealth. Of course, if I wanted or needed her to hold on to a concept for more than a nanosecond, she wouldn't be able.

"I'll pick the restaurant next time," she repeats stubbornly. "I'm not eating this. I'll make something else for my dinner; you can come if you'd like."

Black and White

Above the history shelves
silhouettes of my daughters
flank their black-and-white portrait in soft focus
between the starkness of precise profile.

All of it gone now,
books, hangings,
tenderness, simplicity,
blackened and curled
relegated to the heap of ash and sentimental detritus from fire.

Silhouettes stand out in memory more than portraits,
irreplaceable,
stark,
truth portraits confound.

A window on the shape of a soul we rarely study because we don't
notice.
So busy soaking up the fullfrontal blast we get face-to-face.
Facades.
We miss the raw fleeting nuance of truth in black and white.

<h1 style="text-align:center;font-style:italic">Disguises</h1>

I t was a long-standing tradition in my family that Christmas presents be disguised. Typically, a gift was placed in a box too big or of a different shape than the gift was. Wrapped *things* (it's not quite accurate to call them boxes) began appearing in a corner by the fireplace on the First Sunday of Advent, and the pile grew until Christmas Eve. The whole family went to great lengths to obscure what was inside each package. Gifts were weighted, telescoped, wrapped in separate pieces when possible, and otherwise camouflaged. Outside, the boxes were decorated in beautiful thick papers that my dad brought home from the print shop. Lots of paper companies gifted boxes of wrapping paper at the holidays to their customers. They were heavy and thick, foiled, and embossed, reversible and oh-so-luxurious. You couldn't buy this luxury at the best of stores. I loved running my fingers over them and smelling them; the inks and papers were delicious.

Once wrapped, the package tops were decorated with the fronts of old Christmas cards, along with coordinating ribbons that had been ironed as well as tissue paper and wrapping paper from previous Christmases. Even the ironed papers had a distinct smell of freshly ironed clothes. A comfort smell of home and warmth. Often the cards carried a clue to what might be inside the box. My parents were masters of this game, and guessing began with the placement of each new item. While there was often success or surprise in this little ruse, I had *never* been able to fool my mother.

The year I turned thirteen, I bought a sterling napkin ring with my babysitting money and had it engraved for her. My mother loved the decorative nature of napkin rings, and she loved silver. She used a generic ring while my dad and I both had silver napkin rings passed down through generations with the initials of long-ago relatives engraved on them. They came with stories, and stories got made up to go with them. They carried a lore of their own, which I hoped hers would too, as the years went on.

I gave much consideration to the packaging of this small item. The box in which it arrived was compact, and though not particularly telling, she had guessed so many items in the past, I decided to wrap the small box beautifully and then embed it in something much larger.

My mother had many decorative hanging and ground-level bird feeders throughout our border gardens in the yard, and they were in constant need of filling. I decided an excellent foil would be a large, sturdy liquor case with a garbage bag full of birdseed and the small package buried deep inside.

It was a significant task to find enough paper to cover and decorate the heavy package in the basement without ripping the wrapping paper, then to find a ribbon wide enough to not look like a thong. I chose a card to complement the paper that had a scene of a holiday dinner on it—this was the best I could do for a clue. In the end, I managed to truck that full heavy sucker of a masterpiece up the basement stairs and into the living room in the dark of night while the house was at rest in the first week of Advent.

Her attempts to guess were valiant.

"May I shake it?"

"Yup, it won't break."

"It's so heavy, I can barely move it. What could be so heavy?"

She slid it back and forth across the floor. She tapped it and listened carefully. Nothing.

"It sounds thick and dense."

She guessed clothes, and crystal, and books, and tools. On Christmas morning, she opened the box carefully from the top as instructed to find the mass of birdseed.

"Oh, thank you, sweetheart, for keeping all my birds happy."

Dad and I smiled and moved on. When gifts were done, we sent her back to the box to dig for the small package inside.

"Ooooooh, look! What is it? Oh, wow, after all these years I'm finally a full-fledged Vosburgh; I have my own monogrammed napkin ring."

Dad muttered his usual comment about her being a Vosburgh by injection.

She was delighted. I did it! I had surprised her, *and* she liked it.

The disguises went on for years after but stopped soon after I left home in the way that holidays change as families grow and change. I never stumped her again. Her napkin ring was lost in a house fire years later. But she gave monogrammed silver napkin rings to each of my daughters at their christenings with her initials inside.

An Anniversary

A mid-century marriage put my parents in that post–World War II period when the economy and social status were on the rise. Additionally, my mother had very rigid notions of "proper." While my newlywed parents were of modest means, my mother's notions of etiquette and class ("Money does not class make") drove the train. The 1922 Emily Post was on their library shelf (I bought them a new edition in the seventies, which she scoffed at), though it was not oft consulted. What rules she'd not been raised by, she had memorized for sure. This was the woman who would arrive in the mid-nineties to a Saturday afternoon backyard barbeque baby shower, thrown for us by my husband's family, wearing an elegant silk dress with white gloves and stiletto heels (to show them how it's done), after refusing for weeks to RSVP and threatening not to come because it just wasn't proper for a shower to be thrown by family. When it comes right down to it, Emily Post would not have behaved thus, I'm just saying. My mother was a snob. And I was raised with a silver spoon in my mouth. Quite literally—my baby spoon and fork were from my mother's Reed & Barton Silver Wheat pattern, and they were used on the daily.

My mother loved to entertain, and she did it with great

aplomb, earning a reputation for it. Her table linens and settings were truly lovely, and her exquisite centerpieces (low enough so as not to stifle conversation across the table) always had arranged flowers, usually from her own garden. She put all her traditional wedding presents to good use. I studied at her feet. Some thirty-odd years later, we, too, loved to entertain guests and had many rituals around it that we enjoyed. But our trappings were a bit more modest. The flowers usually came from the grocery store. They were simple bouquets in a simple crystal vase one of our dear friends gave us for a wedding present.

We invited guests to share what we had, even when we had next to nothing. In that first year, in the absence of a table, we had picnic dinners on our living room floor with flowers (always flowers) on an Early Attic side table and served food from the stove. We even invited my mother to join us for similar dinners, though it vexed her something fierce. One did not share one's "poverty" with others. "I eat my meals at a proper table," she'd say. It was a thing of shame.

But we didn't feel impoverished. We felt young and up-and-coming, mindful of what we had, how efficient it was, and how it was sourced. We hadn't yet afforded ourselves a true table for dining, nor did we have the room for it. Years of schooling, one still in school, and only one income—the resultant debt made us cautious. And creative.

My mother was delighted when we told her we were getting married. I had imaginings and some reported reliable information about the kinds of things mothers and daughters fight about when preparing for a wedding. I think my mother was so happy to be marrying me off at the ripe old spinisterial age of thirty that there was no resistance to much of anything. We requested her planning and were grateful when she was thrilled to do it. She honored our minimal wishes (including the blue velvet wedding dress with pockets) and went about the business of making a beautiful evening for us. The flowers she prepared were, as always, exquisite, the meal perfect, and the old, new, borrowed, and blue done with the most thoughtful sentimental touches, some of which she had saved from her own wedding and her mother's before her. Brodie and I couldn't have even thought of other requests. It was wedding perfection. She was absolutely incensed, though, by one thing.

"What do you mean?"

"I think it's silly for us, Mom. Opulent, ostentatious, wasteful, when we've barely a pot to piss in."

"Is that what you think of *me?* Ostentatious and wasteful and whatever?"

"No, Mom, it was a different time. But really, Mom, yours barely gets used a half dozen times a year. That's a lot of bank in the credenza for six times a year."

"That's why you register for it. People buy things as wedding presents you can't afford for yourself. You should choose my pattern. You love it, and then when I die, you'll have a full set that matches."

Indeed, I loved my mother's crystal and china and silver. They were beautiful, and chosen by the two of them, my mom and dad, with nods to abundance and life. At the end of many similar arguments, I escaped both the registry and choosing a china and silver pattern—though I did not escape china and silver entirely. My mother gave us hers for safekeeping after the fire, and we inherited three more sets. In the fifteen-year interim, my mother made it her quest, in the absence of a choice, to make sure we would, at some point in our future of "classless abject poverty," have what was needed to set a formal table.

About a month before our first wedding anniversary, my mother started talking about the most perfect anniversary gift she had found for us. We were allowed twenty questions, per family tradition, but the clues we had left us bereft of any idea. She had us over for dinner just after the turn of the year. The menu consisted of lobster Newberg and the top of our wedding cake, which had been in her freezer for the year. For all my mother's kitchen debacles, she was remarkably adept at crêpes without specific tools to make them. Go figure. The canned Newberg left something to be desired (it was awful) but we appreciated the gesture. There were flowers, of course. They were the same as those we had at the wedding. We sat at the dining room table, and ate off silver, and the holly-patterned holiday bone china, and drank from crystal. She toasted us with champagne.

After dinner was cleared, as we were sipping heated Brandy & Benedictine from engraved snifters, my mother brought out a box, about six inches long and two inches wide, wrapped in forest green with a sprig of variegated holly and white roses on top (our wedding flowers). She allowed us five additional guesses since we'd failed so miserably at guessing, to no avail. She even told us she had never had one of the enclosed and thought we would love it. Her excitement was palpable. I hope we showed proper gratitude in our bewilderment.

The first anniversary, according to whoever makes up these things, is the paper anniversary. Not us, though. Between the two of us we exchanged cards with serious and funny notes. But we now officially refer to our first anniversary as the Anniversary of the Reed & Barton Silver Wheat Solid Sterling Lemon Fork.

February

Hot, Strong, Black

Spending a full day at work with no time for lunch and only an early morning coffee to lean on, then picking up the kids and being in that weary place where even my clothes were annoying me was not a great time to visit my mother. There was little excuse though, when the kids' school was just a quarter mile down the road and when visits meant so much even if she didn't remember I'd been there the previous day and lectured me because she hadn't seen me in years. There would be no disavowing her of this notion. I always apologized profusely and promised to do better. It still made me feel so small and inadequate that I couldn't meet this small desire, even though I was, in fact, meeting it, she just didn't perceive it. *It must feel like years to her.*

They were still working on her medications in the psych unit. Tweaking one thing, changing another. The strings she saw and picked at in the air were hallucinations indicative of overmedication. These adjustments take so much time. Unless the prescriber serendipitously hits the jackpot on the first try, it can be months. We were in it for the long game.

While this old psych unit was more institutional, they were less concerned here about her sleeping habits or the idiosyncrasies brought on by the disease. If she soldiered around at night, they chatted her up. If she took catnaps in a chair at lunch time, they let her be. Clean, coiffed, dressed appropriately, and allowed to *be* —their goals seemed to align more closely with mine. No misery, no aggression. I was grateful she was clean and dry and able to chat up whomever she desired all day and all night. She didn't seem to miss the snow or the gardens.

Yet her deterioration continued. Conversations were increasingly difficult, she was never in her own clothes, she was now in diapers, and she appeared not to know any of us—only that we were familiar. I wondered about the meds and if they were responsible. I wondered why the previous memory care place couldn't affect this change. I wondered if it were just the progression of the disease. I wondered if somewhere in there she hadn't just given up. I wondered what I could have done differently, knowing simultaneously and devastatingly I'd done all I could.

I always found her in the common room, maybe attempting a craft she had never liked or eating a snack—something I could never remember her doing. It was one of the many distressing things about the place for me that made it so much more like prison. All that was familiar and comforting to her was gone, though I didn't know how aware she was of any of it. Her interests were replaced with whatever activities were planned by the director for entertainment. Here, in her jail, there was no flower arranging, no gardening, no sewing, no soft sweet kitty to cuddle. She could knit or crochet, which she hated, or paint with tempera paints, but they would not allow watercolors, at which she was quite accomplished. I guess I could have brought them, but it would have been one more devastating blow if this talent, too, was lost to the tangles in her brain. I was losing her moment by moment. My ever-shrinking mother—what would be left? Meals were what was served by the cafeteria for expediency. She was not served bowls of in-season fresh tomatos with salt and pepper, or spinach straight from the can that she loved, and she wasn't allowed coffee, her drink of choice for any occasion.

She had told me many times that as a child she hated milk. She detested the taste, the way it coated her tongue, and the film it left on the inside of the glass when choking it down was completed. I loved milk.

"I can't even stand putting your milk glass in the dishwasher," she'd say. "The smell and sight of it make me gag. I'm glad you do it for yourself now. Sometimes I made your father do it for me."

Even my milk moustache and milk breath made for queasiness and reminded her of the constant cajoling in her young years to get her to drink it.

The story goes that despite the glasses with different painted animals at the bottom which she was encouraged to guess, she could not be enticed to drink milk. She was wise to the animals and would lift her glass, often spilling it on herself and surrounds to look at the bottom, much to my grandmother's dismay, and exclaim in glee, "This one's the tiger, now I don't have to drink it!"

She was constantly stealing coffee from the adults around her. She preferred the coffee my grandmother drank. Hot, strong, and black. An easy jump to who my grandmother was: strong, silent, with an acid tongue if needed, and thick dark hair. My grandfather, a smooth, charming, handsome man with copious waves of gray hair and piercing blue eyes, drank it with cream and sugar, which Mom would only drink in a pinch when they were trying to find a way to get milk into her. My grandmother was fond of the story and said she just gave up when my mother was five. Black, hot, strong coffee was *all* she drank for the rest of her life. Regardless of the potential exaggerations, it was clear my mother was a black coffee drinker in all her past lives.

This day, in the winter that wouldn't quit, I braved the snow and ice, signed in at the front desk, headed up the elevator, down the hall, and through the locked doors for Cell 4, North Block. As with any day, many of the old souls blocked the doorway and jostled each other to peer through the windows to get glimpses outside the unit where they would never be again. It was soul-crushing on a good day. This day I had stopped at Dunks to get a cup of coffee for Mom because the kitchen and staff refused to serve it, claiming it agitated many residents, and they couldn't do for one what they couldn't do for others.

The nurse at the reception cage shooed the folks from the door and buzzed me in. As always, I was immediately assailed with the smell of stale urine, sweat, chicken soup, old people breath, and despondence. A few steps into the common room, I scanned the residents for my mother's face, her dawn of recognition, and the inevitable smile. I knew she would reach longingly for the cup of coffee, and that I would get the side-eye from the staff and admonishment from the nurses. Not finding her there, I proceeded to her room. She wasn't there either and I headed to the nurse's station, coffee in hand, to see if they knew where she was. "In the common room," I was told, "and coffee is not allowed on the unit."

I went back to the common room and scanned again. No Mom. Looked more carefully now a third time. There she was, hunched over in a chair with her head resting on her knees, vertebrae clear through a turtleneck I did not recognize. I couldn't even be sure she was breathing in that position. Panic stinging down my spine, I rushed over and placed a hand on her too-warm bony dry shoulder. "Mom, it's me. I have coffee for you." It took what felt like forever to rouse her. Overmedicated again. I'd have to speak to the nurses. I'm not sure she even knew I was a familiar face that day. But for the ensuing moments I sat with her while she relished her coffee. "Thank you, thank you, I love my coffee." I glared back at the side-eyes and turned my back to the nurse.

She stopped. "What is she drinking?"

"It's coffee. Hot. Strong. And black."

Poem on the way to work

Oscillations of longing begin the day, and waiting wears the soul.
The toasty deep velvet fragrance calls
gentle warmth spreads through morning-stiff fingers
finally, the soothing sweet,
—sweet relief,
coursing through the whole of me.
Comfort
Calm
Clarity
My core unwinds.
Grab the day, and away.

In crumpled trembling twilight
waiting begins anew.
Weights weigh
Skin crawls
Sheets vex
Stillness eludes
Nightmares
Sweats
Finally thick sleep

just an hour before
the alarm jars into
weary worn wakefulness.
Weather oscillations again before the first distant whiff,
delicious warmth spreading to opposing thumbs
and then,
—then the first sip.

Hot Spiced Peaches

One absolute truth held by all who knew her is that not only was my mother terrible in the kitchen, but she was also downright dangerous. She was not creative with cooking and got easily distracted. She had difficulty boiling water. She often forgot it was on the stove and burned the pot. Stories abound of her failed, burned meals, not the least of which is one that included a salad with sliced tulip bulbs she thought were onions. Even her beloved coffee did not escape. The coffee maker was a mystery to her, always too little or too much of something. Overflows, burnouts, you name it. We tried to get her to refrigerate the excess, but she said she didn't like iced coffee. She made instant. The percolator was a mystery to her and required the extra domestic chore of washing. Being the coffee whore that she was, she stuck with the convenience of instant but still forgot about the water in the kettle. She even burned out ones with whistles. It was only slightly less dangerous for her to make instant. If she succeeded at actually making a mug of coffee, she would carry it with her around the house, eventually put it down somewhere while attending to other busy things, and forget it was there. When she crossed its path hours later, she would be overjoyed to be reunited.

"Oh, good! My coffee."

"Mom, it's cold."

"It was warm once. It's coffee."

But no iced coffee, go figure.

My dad did most of the cooking and meal planning, but sometimes it was left to her. One of my dad's favorite reviews: "Honey! You make me feel like a Greek god, placing before me all these burnt offerings!" He would cackle after saying this for just a bit too long, his own numerous insecurities rising to the surface as he pushed her down in subtle but effective ways, leaving her vulnerable to the next guy after he was gone. She was famous for unpalatable meals where Dad queried: "Do I eat this or have I?"

My dad did the shopping for two reasons: one, my mother was always working and going to night school for a new degree; and two, because she just didn't know what to get. To my dad, the meals he shopped for and the food combinations were obvious from the groceries he kept stocked in the fridge and pantry. But they never planned meals together, so she never really knew what he had in mind. She was supposed to divine the pairings, which contributed to the odd combinations we got. So the hamburger he bought ended up in hamburger and peas on toast, and not as part of the meatballs as he'd intended. Sautéed onions and hot dog coins with paprika served over rice . . . and so it went.

My grandmother was the consummate hostess and cook but she never allowed my mother in the kitchen when she was growing up. Meal preparation was my grandmother's relaxing time. Her meals were spectacular, and she had true culinary talent with influences from the French and Irish sides of her family. Her homemade bread was the essence of comfort—crusty on the outside, dense but light on the inside, just begging for butter and some homemade jam. My mother might have had an easier time with food combinations if my dad had shopped for things with which she was familiar or consulted her on meals. But his influences were German and Italian, and I suspect— though she'd never admit it—asking him was worse than taking the ribbing and cackles that would come as a result. His influences were certainly less fussy, but my mother had no idea what to do with pickled herring or bratwurst and red cabbage.

There *were* things she did well. Her Friday homemade macaroni and cheese was legendary, and her chuck roast done all day in the electric "frypan" was perfect, her cookies brilliant. But when she decided a quarter cup of caraway seeds in mac and cheese would "make it more sophisticated," we revolted. This became the stuff of family legend and fodder for many a joke. She accepted all the teasing and cackling with good nature and a guileless acknowledgement that cooking was not one of her talents. No apology necessary. I think this is how she dealt with my dad's quiet censure. She let him be the cooking star in the family lore and he basked in it. Honestly, the praise heaped on him for a plate of spaghetti and meatballs was fawning and excessive. If I were to speculate now, I would say he basked not only for the praise, but for his tacit judgement that a woman in her time was not proficient in the kitchen.

Before frozen foods and year-round produce were available in grocery stores, we bought commercially canned vegetables and fruits. While canned spinach was liked only by Mom, and canned asparagus was just too nasty for words, canned peaches were palatable, even good. Most of the canned food my mother prepared was simply removed from the can and heated. It was all the same drab color, the same flat taste, and the same slimy consistency. Were I not to eat them as served, they'd be presented to me at the next meal, and the next, straight from the fridge, until they had been consumed. There would be no waste. But peaches responded to canning differently. They were reasonably firm and maintained flavor. My mother would heat them with a couple of whole cloves, a bit of mace, and a shake of cinnamon. She concocted this little side dish on her own and called it "hot spiced peaches."

One day at work, just before my mother went to memory care, my friend Laura mused that she needed to find more creative ways to include fruit on the dinner plate in her young children's meals. I commented in passing about the heated and spiced canned peaches. I further noted that I especially liked them when they were served with rice. It dawned on me that canned peaches were a comfort food for me, though I'd not had them in years.

A few weeks later, Laura left me a message requesting my mother's recipe for peaches. I laughed out loud. "Mother" and "recipe" in the same sentence is a no-brainer for others, but not for me. It occurred to me that Laura had a somewhat distorted notion of who my mother was based on her experience with me and my report of the hot spiced peaches. My mother the cook. My mother the recipe inventor. Highly inaccurate in the grand picture of my mother, and yet, a little nugget of cooking competence and maybe an alter ego she never allowed to shine.

My mother took an almost defensive pride in her "inability" to cook. She thought it said something about her as a professional woman of her time. She had more important things to do than cook. With three graduate degrees and three additional credentials beyond teaching, she was always seeking to learn and improve professionally. She collected competencies and degrees like others collected recipes. She thought it was a good example for me. No need to depend on a man. She would be horrified, and later maybe slightly bemused, that someone thought of her in reference to a viable "recipe." Or not—maybe deep down she'd be pleased.

Now Laura carries my mother's influence to a new generation and I am poignantly amused. I give passing thought to explaining to her that this is not my mother and realize how silly it would seem, and potentially inaccurate. The hot spiced peaches recipe was a wonderful comfort food, and it is a representation of a time my mother was successfully and overtly creative in the kitchen. Laura allowed me to look at her through a different lens and revived and augmented very real and rich memories.

The same evening Laura left the message, I opened my pantry and my eyes went directly to the ever-stocked canned peaches, my own from the previous summer. We had rice as our starch with dinner that night, and I served hot spiced peaches.

"Mom, these are really good!"

"Yes, I've always liked them. I used to mix them with the rice when I was a kid."

"How come we've never had them?"

"I just remembered them. They're a recipe your gran used to make."

Murmurings

Everyone seemed to seek out my mother, either to have her listen to their problems or to receive her advice. The former she did most patiently. The latter only when asked directly and probably more than once. She didn't like giving advice, especially about her friends' children. She would quote my grandmother then: "God should have given us our neighbors' children—then we'd know how to raise them."

For me, the experience was somewhat different. She rarely gave me advice, even when asked. Though she would devote all the time necessary to look at every angle of a situation if I asked her to, I could never discern her opinion. The exception was when she felt she had to lay down parenting boundaries, and that was a simple emphatic command.

"No, you can't go to a party at a friend's house when parents aren't home." She brooked no argument, entertained no discussion. I learned quickly to attempt neither. My dad *always* backed her up. It was their way.

If I sought her out for consolation, I got the what-did-you-do-to-get-yourself-in-this-predicament kind of response. I hated having to defend myself when I was looking for solace.

"Mom, my car got hit in the parking lot today. I'm so mad!"

"Were you parked between the lines?"

"Mom, I got a B in my class. I'm really frustrated."

"Well, I guess you didn't work as hard as you should have."

Listening was another matter altogether. My mother could not avoid judgement when it came to me. When I would share some exciting bit of news—one that made other parents exclaim happily—my mother would respond with a flat, "Oh?"

"Mom, I got a new car!"

"Oh?"

"Mom, I got a raise at work!"

"Oh?"

"Mom, we're having a baby!"

"Oh?"

That one syllable, flat and soft but with a tiny rise at the end, was a cheese grater on my last nerve. A question calling for explanation. I detested the need to justify good news. It always left me feeling as though my good news was disappointing in some way. How could one syllable hold so much?

Eventually, I grew weary of the justifications I thought she needed. I needed something different from her. So I told her I needed excitement when I was excited, and soothing murmurings when I expressed frustration or disappointment. She still didn't really understand, so we came to an agreement. When I called her excited, I would tell her up front that I was excited, and she would respond with: "Oh, how lovely." When I called with any kind of angst, she would offer soothing murmurings.

She thought this was odd and never really got it. She would deliver the agreed-upon phrase for excitement with a laugh behind her voice. I almost thought she was making fun of me, but she wasn't. It was her discomfort with the unfamiliarity of the orchestrated exchange. I hoped it would grow to be more natural.

When I would get through sharing my trials and tribulations with her, in the beginning she would respond with silence. Remembering that her previous types of comments were distressing, she was attempting to give me what I needed. This was awkward, too, but there were no chuckles hiding. Then it clicked. The first time it happened it took me aback.

"Murmur, murmur, murmur."

"Ma, what are you doing?"

"Murmur, murmur, murmur."

"Ma?"

"I'm making soothing murmurings."

We laughed together then, she for her perceived absurdity that this was what I needed, I for my perceived absurdity that she had no gentle words to quiet my angst. I've wondered many times if this were the beginning of the disease or if she had always been this way. I wracked my brain for proof of one or the other with no luck. I must say though, "murmur, murmur, murmur" was far more palatable and made for an easier relationship, maybe for both of us. In the meantime, "murmur, murmur, murmur" has become the go-to in our family when there is nothing to say but we wish to show support. It always engenders even just a skinch of a smile and a loving memory in times of stress.

March

Quarantine

Within the first few days of March, I'm in the elevator heading to see my mother. It stops to let on a nurse who greets me and asks where I'm headed.

"Four North to see my mom."

"Oh, I work there nights. Who is your mom?"

I tell her and encounter what I have experienced for a lifetime.

"I love your mom; she's just wonderful. You're so lucky to have a mom like her."

I could be blind for how far my eyes have rolled back in my head when hearing this, but today it's not old and worn. I am so grateful to this cheery young thing; I wish I could have hugged her there in the elevator. She's the first real live person to indicate to me that she sees my mother as something other than a widget since the beginning of this whole mess.

"She's my favorite! She keeps me company all night long. We talk about all kinds of stuff. Your mom is amazing; I tell her everything. She's such a good listener."

She always was.

"But they should have told you when you signed in, the unit is in quarantine. Intestinal bug. I'm so sorry."

Shit (literally), and I haven't been here for two days.

I consider that notion briefly as the doors spitz open on the nurse's floor and she leaves me with an energetic salutation. As I'm left alone in the box to travel to the fourth floor without exiting and push the button to go back down, I have that relief mixed with guilt I've come to feel about mother visits. Relieved I don't have to find her agitated or miserable. Guilty that I feel relieved. I head back through the lobby and to my car.

Visits are so important to the residents. None of them can hang on to an explanation for why they don't have visitors. "Where is my son?" "Is my daughter coming today?" The questions must be incessant. *An intestinal virus?* (Little would I understand the grief and isolation of quarantine until years later when the world locked down for COVID-19.) I can only imagine the heightened level of cleanup and sterile procedures that must have been necessary to avoid contagion and keep the already perpetually sticky chairs clean in that day. I can only imagine the variety of odors layering with old lady breath and chicken soup. I sink into my relief and guilt, now friends. This one carries more relief: the home says I can't see her. It's not me coming up with an excuse: snowstorm, kids' activities, a cold. I won't have to negotiate the jumble of my mother's cogitations and communications today, or the logistics of finding a clean chair, or the ambient smells.

Incarcerated

When I was in prison
you visited me.

I finally find her
in the crowded common room
slumped over head to knee
bony vertebrae poking up
lending credence to Darwin.

One tiny hand hangs on the sticky floor
and disappears into a sandwich of my own
as I gingerly seek to warm sheer dry tissue paper over phalanges.

After a time she stirs.
Staring vacantly ahead she pulls her hand away
reaches for something only in her distance.

She'll not know me today.

Tell No Secrets

My mother's friends were brilliant and accomplished and kind and giving. Such perfect role models for me growing up. She was a dear and good friend in return. She celebrated success with them and held their hands literally and figuratively through tough times. I never once heard her say a bad word about any of them. She took their calls and was available to them at all hours of the day or night—though they waited until "respectable hours" unless a situation was dire, because that's the kind of women they were. They were there when she married and remarried, and there when her new husband treated her suspiciously. They carefully questioned the black eyes and bruises and grew concerned that she seemed always to be striving to please him about unimportant things, like having to return to a friend's house, alone, in the rain, and later than respectable (he went to bed on return home, and she snuck out when he fell asleep), to fetch a forgotten sweater he had given her so as not to hurt his feelings that it had been left behind.

My mother has taken her friends' secrets with her. She never judged them. If anything, she worried about them. She was always ready to celebrate with them, even when her own heart was breaking. She was so good at secret-keeping that it cost her, in the end, her own health and her own quality of life. She was a private soul and respected others' privacy as well. My mother's friends were her chosen family.

My mother's reluctance to criticize others went far. She was not well liked by her in-laws. They found her odd. She was. And a bit of a social climber. "Money does not class make" was her familiar refrain. They thought my dad would never measure up to her family's expectations. He didn't. On the other side, my dad's family isolated her, keeping her out of inside jokes, not inviting her to events when they could get away with it, and favoring some grandchildren over others. She probably didn't help the situation much in this group of salty "uneducated" types. My mother was proud of her degrees (my dad didn't have one). The more pride she showed, the more they kicked her down. "I don't need no sick-ologist to tell me . . ." would begin the sentences of overstated simplicities after everyone was a few beers in.

They commented once that my younger girl-cousin was going to be the *real* beauty of the family. I think that stuck in my mother's craw and brought out a competitive streak that my dad and I only saw during Monopoly and Scrabble. She was all over me to have a child-modeling career. She managed me to decent local success until I lost my first tooth, such that the proceeds paid for my first year of college. She never told me why she decided to pursue modeling for me, but the timing of my "career" and the fact that I even knew the story of "the real beauty of the family" lends credence to her desire to show off who she and I were without casting shade.

In later years, I saw some of the behaviors from extended family; the slights, the laughter behind hands covering faces, the rolled eyes if she spoke which she rarely did around them, though I saw it often elsewhere (posturing with her jaw jutting just that wee bit and her hand on her waist above her angled hip *just so* for emphasis). It was haughty. I don't think she meant to be openly so; I think she thought she was being a subtle exemplar of what others should aspire to. She never *said* an ill word, and some of it must've hurt. I know it hurt me, for her. And embarrassed me at the same time. I could sense how awkward and called out she felt. But these were my family, and they were just being themselves. I was made of some of the same stuff, and so was my dad. I belonged to them too, didn't I?

By then my dad's relationship with his family had soured and he rarely saw them. By default, my cousins got tons more grandmother-time than I did. Of course, the grandparent I wanted was the one I didn't see. It's hard to say what precipitated the Great Divide. My parents never spoke of it and, when asked, my father told me it was none of my business. When I complained, he told me to shut up. My mother feigned ignorance. I've since made good with my cousins, who are as perplexed as I.

In an effort to keep myself from dying of dehydration or heatstroke in the car, amuse myself, and ferret out some scoop, one day—in heat akin to Death Valley because my mother loved the car heater—I began complaining to her that my cousins got a lot more time and gifts from my paternal grandmother than I did. (I was a horrible, ungrateful, relentless, bitchy tween.) I'm sure this was the time period when my mother began joking: "You should think about being nicer to me or I'll consider retroactive abortion"— (abortion wasn't legal at the time but was discussed often). But it was true; my maternal grandparents spent much more time with me, showered me with treats and took pleasure in granting wishes where possible. That's what all grandparents were supposed to do in my book. What all my friends' grandparents did, I was absolutely sure. And what grandparents did the world over, I assumed.

By my thinking, I should have two sets of doting second-degree relatives. Never mind that my mother's parents had one grandchild and my father's mother had six. This was on the heels of my paternal grandmother sending me a beautiful afghan that she had crocheted for me in my favorite colors with an accompanying note: "With love in every stitch." I tried to give examples of the slights I perceived, knowing I was sounding ungrateful and small in an effort to curry favor and gain information from my mom. I ended my rant with, "She just isn't a very good grandmother."

"Maybe she's the best grandmother she can be" was what I got back, in that this-is-the-end-of-the-conversation tone she had, with an accompanying tone of face. I knew something big had just happened. I knew it right then and there even if I couldn't articulate it. I mulled that conversation over in my head for years before I came to any understanding of its reflection on my mother. I've known it ever since. *Stew on that awhile, petty little girl. This is a life lesson about people and relationships. You've got a lot to learn, and your mom told you more about herself in that one sentence than you could ever hope to gain from your incessant intrusive questions.* My mother gave herself and me and anyone else she loved a day pass. An exemption. An out. I've struggled a lifetime to look through this lens when I feel wronged.

"Maybe she's the best grandmother she can be."

Friends

When I was cleaning out our family home—or, rather, the remnants of it—I found a letter my dad had kept from when my parents were courting. Tucked into a harmonica box, it was a stand-alone treasure because he did not save much. It was also a miracle something he kept had survived because the creep didn't like having my father's stuff around, and my mother threw much away (or lied about from whence it came) to keep him unthreatened. But the prevailing reason for the uniqueness of it was because a house fire had left my mother with what the insurance company considered a total loss. There wasn't much tangible history left. I had never seen this letter my mother had written. They never told me *anything* about this time in their lives, so I was hoping for a romantic scoop. I loved that it was in her own hand. I could feel her, smell the ink, and hear the scratching of her fine nibbed, gray-marbled fountain pen over the paper. Her dad had given her this fountain pen when she was sick with tuberculosis, and she wrote with it almost exclusively every day hence. The love letter to my dad had been written over a period of two days while her friends chided her for being secretive about it. I know those voices.

My mother had yet to introduce my father to her friends, an

apparently common theme for her. They were all on vacation "down the shore" in August '54, only a couple of months after my parents met. Every one of them was a new graduate who had landed a teaching job that would begin the following Tuesday, the day after Labor Day. They called themselves the Fabulous Five, having first gone to Catholic high school, then Catholic college together, and were inseparable. I'd heard so many stories over the years that hinted at their hijinks, but never the whole story of anything. These women knew how to keep secrets. I imagine keeping a relationship from them was not easy. Dad was a Protestant. Not a good thing for a Catholic "girl" in that era.

My mother made reference in that letter to landmarks, movies they'd seen, hot lobster rolls with butter on a flat-sided roll grilled to perfection at a stand (where I would get the same, in the same town I would live in forty-odd years later), sunburns, and playing Scrabble. It intimated their time, their culture, and their place in it. They apparently sat on the front porch of the shore summer home into the wee hours, singing achingly familiar tunes like "Blue Moon," teasing each other, and laughing with abandon. The most poignant thing about the letter though, was the description my mother gave of her friends: describing their looks, their quirks, their talents, and their importance to her. This I know firsthand. This is verifiable. It conjures black-and-white photos of them in my mind's eye, with scalloped white borders, all shirtwaists, pedal pushers, and one-piece bathing suits with pointy breasts, though to my knowledge there are no photos. Little snippet imagery of a casually crossed knee, a cigarette in hand, or a broad grin, leaning against a blue Chevy with fins or lounging on the porch. These were the elusive surreal halcyon days of their lives, before marriage, children, careers, Sputnik, Khrushchev, a dead president, the Civil Rights Movement, The Cold War, teenagers, ageing parents, and the myriad complications that relationships bring as we age and grow and change. The letter was a slice of the innocence of their time, the pull and tug of a new relationship when separated, the deliciousness of keeping something just for oneself, and the abject importance of a group of women to have by one's side.

I made copies of the letter and sent it to each of "the girls" with a note explaining how I'd found it. They all sent a note back (of course they did), thanking me for the memories and the window on my mother, and adding something to the story it told. All handwritten thank-you notes with perfect Palmer script. The snapshots became clearer to me, digital with turquoise, cerise, and sienna. My mother's friends are amazing women and amazingly great role models even now.

Dignity

My mother was proud and dignified. She never swore, never let on if she were feeling peaked, and never strayed from Emily Post (obsolete though her edition may have been). There was a different fork for everything (and if you used the wrong one, you didn't go to heaven); a baby shower for your child was thrown by someone else; wine only tasted right from the appropriate wine glass, which was, of course, why they were shaped that way; fights were never instigated at your in-laws'; and white was never worn between Labor Day and Memorial Day.

She was diagnosed with breast cancer when she was in her fifties, a year almost to the day after my dad died. Her main concern during treatment and recovery was her dignity. To her that meant no nudity in or out of hospital, no medical discussion except with the doctor—alone, and no frumpy sick face or clothes. Sickness was shameful and happened in private, as it had been in those early teen years when my grandmother nursed her back from TB, and they told the world she had scarlet fever.

Her treatments were on Tuesdays every third week. She managed to keep her hair, and though she shared her diagnosis with some, during the two days after her chemotherapy that she spent sleeping on the bathroom floor to be near the toilet to puke, she saw no one and accepted no help of any kind. She planned her at-work schedule around the days she would be incapacitated and completed work at home on recovery days. She never stopped. Thursdays began the recovery, and that was my cue to get food to the house that I knew she could enjoy and tolerate. She accepted no callers, and I had to beg her just to open the door so I could give her a gentle hug. I'd been admonished not to use my key. Usually, I was only allowed to leave my packages on the table on her lovely genteel three-season porch. She tolerated my soups well and looked forward to the lavender soaps and bath salts I left for her when she felt up to it. This was the most she'd let me do for her, which was a great source of frustration for me. I'd have moved right in with her, held her head over the toilet, wiped her face with a cold cloth. I wanted to care for her and was hurt by her pride.

She would weather the entire experience on her own, just as she had weathered tuberculosis as a freshman in high school. When chemo was all done a year later (due to some delays from winter upper respiratory complications), she re-emerged on a regular schedule and life resumed as though it had all never happened. Woe to you if you brought it up.

Years later, on a fine summer day when Helen and Lillie were preschoolers, Mom was sitting at the end of the dock at our lake house in a modest bathing suit that gave no hint of the scars inside or out, and out came the non sequitur, "If I had to do it over, I wouldn't. It was just too awful." To say I was shocked was an understatement, though I gave no indication. This was a new side to my mother the fighter. I had never seen anything knock her down. She did not often initiate intimate conversation, so I knew to keep my silence and let the story come to me. She didn't go much further except to note that the loss of her health and the physical devastation was just too much to bear without my father.

While it hurt that she would not allow me the role of care-giver, which I had desperately wanted to do for her, I understood the priority and intimacy of their relationship from my own years of history with them. The two of them, my mom and dad, stood shoulder to shoulder. They didn't allow others in. It was them against the world. I asked my mother once if she loved me best in the whole world. She said no; she was married to my dad, and it was him she loved most. She loved me very much, she said, but my dad was at the top of her list. They kept each other's secrets, had inside jokes, and she'd have allowed him to care for her under these circumstances, but her need was not an intimacy she would ever share with me.

During the ensuing years, she would watch her grandchildren grow and teach them to read, and draw, and arrange flowers, and read poetry. She would have her implant replaced three times because it burst. She would retire. She would build her floral business. She would remarry. She would rebuild her home. The guy she married was creepy and made us all uncomfortable. Nothing we could do; we supported her choice. I got asked by her friends about some of the more obvious decisions she was making during those years. There were hints she questioned her own judgement about this suitor. She kept him hidden for a long time. She didn't want to introduce him to her friends, fearing what they might think because he was many years her junior. I suggested she might want to examine her reluctance carefully.

Shortly after they married, holidays were moved to our house. I always called my mother to ask if there was something special they would like to honor tradition or request for the meal. One year at Easter, my mom requested grilled asparagus, which was in season and which she loved. I told her I was sure the Easter Bunny would leave some for her. She was delighted that I had it in my garden and expressed her pleasure when the bowl was passed to her at Easter dinner. The creep took this opportunity to loudly proclaim in front of family, friends, and all our grade school offspring in attendance that "in deference" to my mother he would "not partake of asparagus because it makes semen taste disagreeable." My mother turned a deep red, whispered "oh, no" and left the table, tripping over her own feet. She sequestered in the guest bedroom to compose herself. "Well, it does," he interjected into the ensuing silence. She returned sometime later when the conversation had moved on and the rest of the folks were speaking just a bit too brightly, and did not speak for the rest of the meal. I knew the body language. The lips pressed thin, shoulders back, spine ramrod straight, and hands nested Emily Post-style in her lap. They were arguing in whispers when they left as soon as the dessert and coffee were over. She insisted (almost stomped her foot) on leaving, though he wanted to stay. "Who can we talk to about it if we can't talk to them?" he yelled once they were outside. I heard my mother growl for the first time in my life: "No one. NO! ONE!"

At that time, her friends would call me from time to time, expressing distress at her behavior and isolation, and her responses when they tried to talk to her about their concerns. She had come to believe her situation with him wasn't good, wasn't supportive, wasn't equal, but she hadn't the skill anymore to extract herself from it. Her pride wouldn't allow for requests or acceptance of help. She was ashamed. She had lost her ability to plan and execute. But even in her advanced stages, she somehow managed to cover for him or her own waning balance, out of pride or self-preservation, or simply poor judgement. Explanations for black eyes were "None of your business" or "I fell off my Harley," which of course she didn't own but thought it disarming to say. Her friends went crazy over those explanations; they were angry, worried, and they wanted someone to fix it, which they made exceedingly clear. Such good women friends my mother had. They truly cared and truly hurt for her.

She prevaricated to the fire chief and arson investigators when the house burned down, save for the flagstone floor of the three-season porch. We all followed her lead, including him, and did the same when asked about his smoking; we did this for *her,* allowing her to believe what she needed to. The fire started right by the back door where he kept an ashtray on a shelf. She didn't allow him to smoke in the house and he often had a drink and a cigarette before retiring. The losses were not just internal. The firefighters, out of necessity, trampled flowerbeds and killed specimen mountain laurel and indigenous pink dogwood. One could hardly ask them to step gingerly between the violets and petunias and make sure they didn't knock over the lilies with their hoses when they were literally trying to avoid a potential forest fire. They investigators asked her if there were any way he could have left a lighted cigarette on the porch, her favorite room. "No," she insisted, "he's very careful."

It was eventually determined it was an electrical spark that started the whole thing a very short time after he went to bed in his drunken state on that sultry summer night. Evidence for it was weak, though there did not seem to be another explanation since he was "very careful." He was still drunk the following morning, even though he'd no access to alcohol the entire night as the house burned and the firefighters labored to ensure the surrounding trees and brush did not catch. My mother lost a lifetime of memories that night and a home she held on to, though it was too big, as her last connection to my dad. He lost his computers and gaming consoles. He had very few other possessions. They would rebuild, but she was never again comfortable there and said she missed my father's presence. After this we would all become frustrated at times with her intermittent lack of memory and focus, and her new intense propensity for disorganization, which we chalked up to a combination of chemo-brain and trauma. I quietly acknowledged her ten-year cancer-free anniversary when she called one evening. Silence. Heartbeats. Too many.

"Mom?" I pressed.

"I have it again," came a little voice almost too soft to hear.

She'd had a mammogram on her remaining breast and two lumps were found. They had been biopsied. She'd had a consult with the oncologist. Two different kinds of cancer, and both different from the cancer ten years ago.[1] The oncologist had told her they wouldn't treat her aggressively because of her age. Argument ensued. She wanted aggressive treatment, "like they'd do for any thirty-year-old." She prevailed. She saw the oncology surgeon, discussed reconstruction. Consulted the plastic surgeon. Set a date and had a schedule for chemotherapy. All alone. She had told no one, including me, until I brought it up.

When I asked her about aggressive treatment and what it meant, how it was different, she said she felt the oncologist was dismissive of her and her life's meaning because of her age, and she would "not be treated thus." That was the mother I knew. I went into high gear planning soups and shopping for bath products to be ready for her after surgery. The creep only ate food from restaurants with rare exception, so it would be important to make sure she had things on hand as she would not be up to going to restaurants, though he continually pushed her to do so, from the day she got home from the hospital.

The surgery went well, but she developed a fever on the second day of recovery and was sent back into surgery to clear an infection. The creep visited her the night after surgery; otherwise he did not come to the hospital. I brought her home when she was finally released, because he was at work (he still had a job then), and settled her with painkillers, which she refused to take—didn't want to get addicted—and antibiotics. Her chemo was scheduled to begin in six weeks. The process had changed significantly in ten years, and she was informed she would lose her hair by the second round. Our children donated hair. Wigs were purchased.

Her first evening home, he stopped on his way from the office and picked her up a Big Mac from McDonald's. She ate about half and went to bed. He put the rest in the fridge for later. What

---

1. Incidence has risen ~1%/year in the 2010s–2021, with faster increases under age 50. American Cancer Society. *Breast Cancer Facts & Figures 2024–2025*. Atlanta: American Cancer Society, 2024.

the fuck? Cold McDonald's. Maybe high food, but not sick food. He went to work the next day, and I called her on schedule for her meds to ensure she took them. She said she wasn't eating and only drank enough to get her antibiotics down. When I called around dinnertime, he said she was sleeping and couldn't talk.

"She didn't eat anything all day," I said, "nor did she drink. I'm concerned."

"I'm not worried," he replied blithely. "It looks like she had a couple bites of her Big Mac from last night. I'll have a glass of wine with her later." On painkillers? He had no idea she wasn't taking them.

He thought she would want to go out to dinner with him but realized that might "have to wait a day or two." He went on with nonchalance to tell me she was so exhausted that she had attempted the stairs in the house sometime during the day, only to tire and stop to rest. He found her asleep curled up midway on a tread when he got home. He thought it was amusing and cute. I was devastated for her. By the second day home she was getting worse rather than improving. My radar was up, and I made plans to call her the next morning with an invitation to come stay with us. I knew she would refuse as she had so many times in the past, but I had to try. I could take care of her easily in the flow of family life, but I was unable to leave my grade schoolers to go care for her at that point in time. Being a sandwich generation, I had responsibilities above and below me.

I was frustrated to tears that night when telling Brodie about the creep's wicked lack of concern and responsibility toward my mother and her health. "Go get her!" was his directive. I was afraid. Afraid she'd be mad and the creep would resist and keep her from me. "Let her be mad and safe," Brodie said.

I called at nine o'clock the next day. "Morning, Ma."

"Oh. Hi, honey," came the weak response.

"You don't sound awake, you okay?"

"I must've needed rest. I've been sleeping since yesterday afternoon. I didn't even get up for dinner."

"Did you take your meds, Ma?"

"No, I slept right through them."

Now in rescue mode, I mustered all my courage (because Brodie said I had this) and *told* my mother I was on my way to come get her, and that she should pack a few comfortable things so she could stay a few days until she felt better. The tiny little voice on the other end of the phone sounded ancient and feeble. "Okay." My husband had been on point. I'd done the right thing, though I couldn't ever recall a time I told my mother to do anything. Such is the ingrained nature of our mother-child roles.

She was in a chair by the porch door when I arrived, wearing the same robe and pajamas that I had left her in two days prior. She hadn't the energy to pack, so I asked what she wanted and packed for her. It was with much support and very slowly that I got her to my car right outside the porch. She slept for the thirty-minute drive to my home. It was not lost on me that I had done more to assist my mother in those few minutes than she had ever allowed me.

I got her to the black rocking chair in the living room and opened the windows overlooking my gardens and the lake, letting in the breeze and hum of spring. She promptly fell asleep again. She felt hot to me, so I drew her a bath with lavender bath salts, lavender soap, lavender candles, a large terry robe, and lavender-colored towels. I prepared gauze and tape to change her dressings and gently woke her. "Oh! A bath. A bath always makes me feel better." I kept my eyes shut to assist her getting in the tub. She'd never wanted me to see her naked. I told her I'd stay close by in case she needed something. "Oh, that's a good idea, thank you." Now the alarm bells were really going off. A good idea? She was *asking* for help.

She called for assistance (holy shit) getting out of the tub, which, again I did with my eyes closed, and helped her into the big fluffy robe, shuttered likewise. "Sarah, I was able to take off the front bandage, but the back one I can't reach, will you help?"

They had taken skin from her back to make enough up front for her implants, and there was a long incision there.

"Ma, have you changed this bandage? It's very yellow and the tape is black and stuck."

"No, I haven't. I couldn't reach."

Come to find out, the creep wouldn't help with her dressings because he didn't want to see her wound. She was so objectified he was afraid it would impact how he felt about touching her body going forward. (He constantly took photos of her breasts from above in low cut blouses and attempted to share them with us.) I wanted to scream and punch him in the face and vomit. For those moments, I studiously concentrated on what she needed to keep the contents of my stomach on the inside. My weakened mother, who had made it through cancer all by herself the first time, couldn't rely on him for a simple dressing change because he only wanted to see and know her perfect plastic breasts.

I soaked the bandage. It was crusty with a foul odor. Despite the generous soaking, I pulled off bits of skin with the tape and gauze to reveal a hot, red, swollen, running infection underneath. No wonder she wasn't feeling well. I soaked it more, medicated and dressed it, and left her to maintain her dignity, dress the other incision in front, and dress herself in clean comfortable clothes that I had laid out for her. She was exhausted from the bath, the dressing, and the trip. I helped her stretch out on my living room couch to nap, but not before I made her call the doctor. We made an appointment to see him the following morning.

In the meantime, I indicated the nature of her recovery to the creep in a phone call. He was unconcerned since I had it "all under control." My girls doted on their grandmother, and she accepted all they brought her to eat and drink. What grandmother could refuse a grandchild who says, "I made this for you!" The girls were plenty old enough to be in on it. My mother didn't usually drink, except coffee, so they made and brought her Jell-O, homemade sorbet, and consommé, all of which they set up beside her chair with their own tea sets replete with dishes and silverware and napkins with rings and ate along with her. There was method to my madness.

The doctor changed her antibiotic, and the infection began to clear. She called our family attorney in the following days as she felt stronger and had time to think. She wanted a divorce. I managed to hold my tongue, knowing it could go a thousand different ways. I brought her back home when she felt better. She told him she wanted a divorce that evening. "You can't throw me out like an old pizza box," he protested. She had no counterargument prepared, and he wore her down. He wasn't leaving anytime soon.

And it was over, just like that. My ability to help, the inside look at his neglect. Her time with us, if referred to again, was only as a little respite at the lake to recuperate and give him a break because he had to work.

Years later, in the time of her incarceration, he told me one day when I called to update him on her progress or lack thereof in the memory unit that *he* was thinking about divorcing *her* so he could "go on with my life." He visited her just once in the Community Home, on their wedding anniversary. By then he was dating someone his age and wanted to remarry.

She was still useful to him at home, though. Bruises to her dignity were part of his repertoire, and I was bereft of understanding why she tolerated it. It was all I could do to be civil to the man. About two weeks before she left for the memory care unit, he had answered the phone one morning when I called. His voice was hoarse, and I politely asked after his health as my mother would expect me to do. He reported that he was not sick; he had been up all night yelling at her to "set her straight," but it was worth it "because our makeup sex was fantastic this morning." Had my mother known he'd said this to me, she'd have wanted the earth to swallow her. The nature of that comment brought bile to my throat. Many a time my parents had argued, and he could be cutting, but my father had never raised his voice to her, nor she to him. Witnessing the disrespect for my mother and her dignity, I screamed and pounded one fist into the other hand only to end up with red fingers in a puddle of anger and frustration in my husband's arms. We had sought help everywhere—our church, protective services, the town social worker, motor vehicles, her doctor—but she always managed to be in control and articulate enough that no one believed the depth and breadth of her decline, or his advantage.

She did his bidding regularly, the antithesis of the oppositional mother I knew. She put up no fight, with rare exception. Apparently available for makeup sex, she still drew the line at money. He didn't work for the last five years of her life, nor did he appear to try to find a job. Their finances were separate, but he had no money. He never had. He also had few expenses. He spent what he made and kept no savings. She asked nothing from him for the upkeep or running of the house, as instructed by her attorney. He badgered her regularly to write him checks from her home equity account off her house that was paid in full.

Years later, when she left for the memory unit and I had the checkbook, it was too late. Between his spending and the Great Recession when her house lost significant value, there was nothing left but bills when she died. As it were, when she was still home and she obliged him with a check, he used the money to purchase the things she wouldn't buy for him; alcohol, gaming equipment, more computer stuff, and eating out, which she considered a waste of money. She thought he drank to excess. She had kept track for years in a little notebook with measurements in fractions of inches from the bottom of the bottle to the meniscus of the spirits, until she forgot how. She attended Al-Anon meetings to try to figure out how to fix him but abandoned them when she realized working that program was about her and not him. He had a half dozen computers/consoles and they always needed something new or updated, the latest and greatest. It was a dance they did like boxers in a ring of an unfair fight; they circled and circled, but he got the knockout as soon as the bell rang and she threw her first punch. She never stood a chance. Once she wrote one check, he began angling for the next. She complained about it to me but always gave in. He was a kept man and loved it. There was no preservation of her dignity, let alone consent in her house, and I was as powerless as she.

April

Quarantine

I call every day now before heading over to the Community Home, as the intestinal bug quarantine drags on. It's not been good. They're having trouble containing it. Sometimes I call again at night after shift change to check in and get the sweet nurse from the elevator, who gives me a cheery update. My mom has not been sick. The nurse will even put Mom on the phone if she's hovering nearby.

"Hey, Mom, it's me."

"Hello?" She's tentative. "Fancy hearing from you?"

"My pansies by the back door are looking lovely; they have tons of blooms. I even picked a bunch and put them in a vase."

"Are the violets up?"

"They sure are, and very happy this year. The *Muscari* is covering the lawn when I drive by the college."

"Who is this?" I hear faintly. She is handing the phone back to the nurse. I got two exchanges about flowers; It's a good night.

Me & She

My adolescent days full of sniping
frustration
falling short.
Couldn't talk without a fight.

Still, she always said
wake me when you get home
so I know you're safe
I'll go right back to sleep.

But in those nights
too beautiful to leave her be
I'd find her hand
soft, warm, tiny in mine,
and pull her gently from sleep as if tempering taffy.
Connected we'd pad in silence
to the backyard, my mother and me.

Softcool freshcut grass
heady riotous nectars
a clear full moon high

at perigee
crickets calling.
Her midsummer gardens transformed.
Enchanted silver.

Our hands clasped tightly
we'd not speak out there
on the way back to our bedroom hallway
or in the following hazy summer morning brightness
thick with cicadas' undulant song
announcing the heat to come.
Gardens Kodachrome then
as though those wee hours
merely an argent dream of awe and intimacy.

Neanderthal Woman

The quarantine in the unit from the intestinal bug *(ugh!)* leaves me with reminiscences of other springs with my mom. Mostly they center on our gardens and the many hours my mother and I enjoyed them. But this day, the spring anticipation brings memories of another time of waiting for our firstborn.[1]

"I want to be in the delivery room when the baby is born," my mother said at Sunday brunch in the seventh month of my first pregnancy. Not "Would you like me to be?" or "Can I be helpful?" Nope, just a demand. She had a baby once in the fifties in a state of medically induced unconsciousness, so of course, she knew best. She'd been full of "helpful little tips" all along, but this was a new level of invasion. Mostly I said, "Oh, thank you" and moved on, careful not to roll my eyes in her line of sight.

"Your grandmother was there to greet you when you were born. She was the first to hold you. I want to be the first to hold my grandbaby. It's a family *tradition*."

---

1. A version of "Neanderthal Women" was first published in *What Just Happened? Shaking the Tree – brazen. short. memoir.* (Vol.6), edited by Marni Freedman and Tracy J. Jones, published by Memoir Writers Press, 2025.

Fucking presumptuous. "We will make sure you are there too," I acquiesced reluctantly. How could I leave my poor widowed mother out of this? We were all she had left.

"We?" she asked. "Too? *He's* not going to be there, is he? Why? He'll never think of you the same again if he sees all *that*." She gulps her coffee as though she's had nothing to drink in weeks. "Besides, you won't hold her right away; you'll be knocked out for several hours. I will take care of the baby while you come to and make yourself presentable. That's what your grandmother did for me."

My grandam was a delivery room nurse in a time when women were put under, anesthetized during labor. While I was sure mid-1990s delivery room staff were used to take-charge grandparents, they'd not met my mother. I did not want them distracted with the occupation of Ms. I-Know-How-This-Should-Be-Done or worse, having to ask her demanding self to leave.

"Mom, Brodie's going to be there because he's the dad, and my husband and birth coach. They are not going to put me out."

"Birth coach?" she scoffed. "Honestly. How ridiculous. The doctor takes care of all that."

I should have told her *she* was the ridiculous one.

"You need to take advantage of modern medicine," she continued, barely coming up for air. "There is no reason to be so barbaric and endure all that pain."

Oh boy. She was just clueless. She had been rolled into the delivery room straight from church, coiffed, in her Sunday best with stilettos and gloves, and given medication to induce full-on, put-you-out anesthesia. She woke up shaved, stitched, clean, and fresh with a baby in the nursery. When she was released from the hospital, she dropped me off at Gramma's for a few hours, likewise accessorized, having set her hair the night before, in a shirtwaist dress with the belt on its tightest notch (because she "kept her figure" with a net weight loss) so she could go check the sales at Lord & Taylor.

"Mom, it's how most babies are born these days," I explain. "It's considered healthy for baby and mom."

"Who is this doctor you have? You should ask him about having you put out. Then you don't have to be embarrassed when they shave you, and you won't feel it when they sew you back up."

I didn't even know what to say. I didn't want to argue about shaved nether regions, anesthesiology, and episiotomies with my mother, now or in labor. Or *ever*.

"Mom, I'm going on the advice of my doctor, Amy. I would love to have you there, but you'll need to be supportive." By now my chest was hard and tight, my breathing shallow. I felt my head swim from lack of oxygen.

"Of course, you have a *woman* doctor. *That's* what this is all about."

Are you fucking kidding me? I wanted to say, but she was my mom. I tried to be gentle.

"Mom, after making her and carrying her and birthing her, it is her father and I who will hold her first. We will happily hand her over to you after I nurse her."

"Why are you shutting me out? This is my grandchild . . . Wait! Nurse her? You're doing that too? This woman doctor is making you one of those militants. They can give you pills to dry up your milk. You don't have to go through all of *that*. You don't want to get saggy breasts! It's so primitive."

I focused on the tinkling and hum of the café, using it as a kind of ostinato to calm my breathing.

"Mom, if you would like to be in the delivery room, I'm happy to make it happen. Would you like us to call you when we leave for the hospital or when delivery is closer?"

"What do you mean, closer?"

"It's my first baby and it may take a while for things to move along. We can play Monopoly." This was her favorite game; she was absolutely cutthroat.

"Well, I don't want to be waiting around all day being *friv-*

olous; I'm busy. They can give you medicine so it's quick. Why are you insisting on being so crass, so philistine?!"

I tried for slower, deeper breaths. Not easy, especially with a baby in there. "We'll call you when it's imminent, Ma."

Her next words, all quickly pressed and run together as if they were one, carried panic behind her annoyance. "Never mind, this is ridiculous. You haven't listened to anything I've told you. You'll never get your body back. No one knew *I* was pregnant until eight months because I wore a girdle."

A bite of over-easy egg mid-swallow threatened to stick as the rush of anxiety brought on by my mother's judgement layered over my relentless morning sickness and shallow breathing. Her eyes were bulging and pointedly staring. Silence. Swallow.

I sipped tea and attempted another nibble of dry toast to push the egg down. But my mother wasn't finished. "You're already so big, you'll never have a flat stomach again, you won't look good in clothes, and your vagina will be loose. Do it the way I did, and you won't feel a thing. When they sew you up, it'll be tighter than a virgin." Wound up, and almost yelling now, she said, "Why won't you take advantage of modern medicine? We live in the twentieth century. You should not be having a baby like a Neanderthal woman!"

I never finished breakfast, about which she was happy. Must stay trim, after all. From then on, I studiously avoided anticipatory birth comments when my mother was nearby. I was sad not to share this joyful anticipation with her but was relieved she would not be in the delivery room. I knew my decision made her feel rejected. She would never understand, but the desire to do best by my baby gave me the courage to stand up to her intrusiveness.

We did call my mother when we left for the hospital, and we told her we'd keep her posted. She expressed displeasure and censure on subsequent updates about how long things were taking. When I called with the last update—between close contractions—to let her know her grandbaby's arrival was imminent, her response was simple: "I'm so busy; I'll get there as soon as I can."

Four days of labor later, after a plunger finally extracted a stubbornly reluctant neonate, my girl was born. Our new babe was bathed, swaddled by nurses, and placed in my arms. The complications just minutes ago seemed in the distant past.

Brodie lay on the bed next to me, our daughter nestled safely between us. We were dressed in old T-shirts and sweats. I was comfortable and content, even with a messy, sweaty ponytail, loose vagina, and saggy belly. Milk-drunk, exhausted, and warm, our babe cared not. We greeted her and said her name to her. Helen. We told her the story that went with it and sang or recited poetry as we had when she was on the inside. We changed her first diaper in great haste to stop the little newborn chirps of distress she expressed and resettled right quick into a three-way cuddle.

My mother made it to the hospital just a couple hours after birth, flowers in hand, in a reverent hush. She was in awe of her granddaughter, instantly smitten, shedding a tear or two, as I handed her our sleeping babe, whom she held alternately close and at a distance, gazing at her face, depositing whispers of kisses on her crown, counting her fingers and toes, exclaiming over and over in her ear, "I wish your grandfather were here." Mom's small sighs were as warm and sweet as the sighs of the new babe. Hours and the world melted away. She rocked and sang as she had done for me so many years ago. And we were able to rest.

Days later our new little threesome sat on the couch at home. My husband leafed through the processed and printed photos from the hospital whose arrival we had anxiously awaited, as I nursed and inspected them over his shoulder. We had fun exclaiming over details and nuance we'd already forgotten. The pictures of my mom and my girl were lovely.

"Honey, go back," I said to him. "Is that what I think it is?" There it was: my mother's familiar waist-front fanny pack. Barely concealed was the unmistakable faint outline of a 9 mm semiautomatic handgun. My mother, serene as could be in my maternity room with my hours-old daughter in her arms. *Militant, Mom?* I don't know if it was a passive-aggressive move on her part or just habit. I lean toward the former.

Breeding

In the blink of an eye (*den Augenblick*, as my dad would say), I find myself a grown adult, four years into my marriage, and still apologizing to my mother like a little girl for some minor infraction that annoys adults but is a curiosity to kids. My mother's first reaction upon being told we were expecting: "But I'm too old to be a grandmother."

"She can't call me Grandma. I will not be called Grandma. And don't expect me to be your free babysitter; I'm too busy for that and I have my own life. I'll help out when I can, but you won't take advantage of me. I see that happening with all my friends, and it's not going to happen to me. I have a life."

"Sorry, Ma. Sorry. No, we won't. Sorry."

She was relentless. This was worse than the "Oh?" I usually got when presenting good news. By the by, my mother reconciled herself to her grandmotherhood and fell in love with her grandchild. She was usually too busy to help with babysitting, though we gave her plenty of opportunities. Some of that had to do with the unsecured and loaded guns she kept at the ready around her house and on her person in a fanny pack when she left home. She did not like coming to our house to sit because it was too far (thirty minutes, no weapons), and we did not allow our daughter in her home without us because she would not secure her firearms.

"Why are you so neurotic about this? I'm a responsible gun owner who has been trained to shoot."

"Responsible owners lock them up around kids, Ma. Besides, it's state law. High, dissembled, trigger locked, and ammo stored and locked elsewhere. I'll buy you a lockbox and trigger locks."

"No, you will not! I'll not feed into this ridiculous, paranoid, irrational behavior."

I shed many a tear over these details and the loss of intimacy with her grandchild but remained steadfast. She never missed an opportunity to let me know how deeply I was hurting her and how mentally unstable she thought I was.

"Why are you shutting me out of your life like this? It's cruel. I'm your mother. This is my grandchild."

In public, it was all about smiles and tight family relationships. She delighted in telling others we had a legacy going because she was an only-child girl, I was an only-child girl, and I had an only-child girl. To my mom a legacy, to me a childhood of loneliness. We did not bother to correct her presumptions. What would happen would happen. Pregnancy and I did not get along, and I struggled with morning sickness such that after delivery I had a net loss of weight. She was sure we wouldn't have more children, both for how sick and difficult pregnancy and labor had been and to carry on her "legacy."

When we first confirmed we were expecting our second baby, we were less excited to tell her. I ended up hospitalized with morning sickness (hyperemesis gravidarum—extreme morning sickness). I had become dehydrated as I could not keep down even ice chips. We avoided her disapproval and withheld the news longer, waiting until things had settled down. They didn't. The doc became suspicious I was carrying twins as the calculated conception date did not normally make for sufficient hormone levels to have such rocking hard morning sickness. They were worried about a complicated pregnancy in a "geriatric patient."

Good lord, I was thirty-seven. The doc scheduled me for an ultrasound. Twins! We alternated between excitement and terror about changing from a family of three to a family of five. We were going to be busy parents with two newborns and a two-year-old.

We arrived for our ultrasound, nervous, and me still sick, but without worry. The sonographer kept a placid face as always while she hydroplaned about my belly on the cold film of jelly. We were impatient to hear a heartbeat, and it seemed to take forever. Abruptly the sonographer professionally informed us the doc would be in to talk to us and left the room with crisp efficiency.

This was not the same as with our firstborn. I had heard the heartbeat and seconds later they turned the screen to show me my girl. Now I convinced myself the sound was turned off.

The doctor entered quickly, though the time between the exit of one professional and the entrance of another seemed interminable. She too skated around my belly.

"We are unable to locate a fetus," she said.

The ultrasound yielded what appeared to be an empty womb.

"You will likely spontaneously miscarry 'products of conception.' I can assure you this happens in potentially 25 percent of pregnancies. Before ultrasound, women never even knew it. It won't affect your fertility." She matter-of-factly told us the name of the kind of pregnancy it was. Neither of us remembered.

The doctor continued, "If you don't miscarry within the week, I have you scheduled for another ultrasound for a week from today where we will double-check. If we still cannot locate a fetus or fetal cardiac activity, then we'll perform a D&C procedure."

Procedure. Products of conception. So sterile. Cold. So nonhuman. Our heads spun. My stomach flipped. From twins to nothing in seconds.

That may have been the longest week of our married life to date. We had kinda wrapped our heads around a family of five. We were disappointed at best, but really in mourning. To us the pregnancy was real, and the two babies in there were ours. Two little sibs for our firstborn. Two new squishy, pruney, newborns, sweet-smelling little loves to complement our family. I'm not sure how we got through the week. I know we tried to distract ourselves, but every time I used the bathroom, I expected blood where I didn't want it. As the week wore on and no blood came, we both had that horrible mixed hope and dread that added to the ever-increasing stomach roiling and loss of weight.

The week ended and the pert, efficient, blonde sonographer, whose bob always looked fresh cut and whose classic dresses looked as though wrinkles ran from them screaming into the night, called for me from the waiting room. I was in sweats, a T-shirt, and a messy bun, eyes still red from the morning of tears. We both got up to follow her.

"He can wait outside the door." She indicated my husband with the back of her hand flipped in his direction, as though he were superfluous.

"But . . ."

"I'll call him in shortly, after I complete measurements and calculations."

They had not done this before. It took forever. I was as alone as I had ever felt. When she finally invited him in, he said, "That sounds like a heartbeat." I was so terrified and so frozen I hadn't even noticed. It was then she turned the monitor so we both could see our little camera-shy singleton. A tiny peanut with arms and legs waving at us. Relief. Tears. Joy. Excitement. And more vomiting to come.

The ride home was full of happy tears, anticipation, and relief. Curiously, my mother was waiting at our front door, banging on the door knocker and calling our names frantically. The police were there. She was close to hysterical. She was irrational, even. We were confused and annoyed by her behavior, especially in our somewhat overwhelmed state—so many emotions over such a short time. Now I know we were seeing the early manifestations of the disease, but back then we just saw her as intrusive.

My mother had been too busy to sit that morning, so our toddler was with a neighbor. But I figured she knew we wouldn't be home, given that we'd asked. She had no idea where we were going, and we had not told her. She was not too busy, however, to call the police for a wellness check and drive over to meet them at our house because she had been unable to reach us.

Armed with the first ultrasound pictures, we pulled into our driveway, not even noticing the police, and ran to her to tell her the good news, proffering the photos. We tripped over each other's sentences, trying to get the whole sequence of events out. She listened, stone-faced and rejecting, pushing the filmy paper back toward us.

"I couldn't reach you. I was worried. Where were you? Why didn't you answer? I couldn't reach you. I couldn't reach you."

It was almost intoned.

"Mom, we asked you to babysit this morning; you knew we would be out."

She didn't skip a beat. "Well, if it were twins, you would have had to abort. As it is, you're breeding them like rats."

Man with a Full Career

"You're just like me. You're going to need a man with a full career."

I'm nothing like you, and I'm never gonna be.

"You're going to have interests that you want to pursue, and a career yourself. You're not going to want a man clinging to you, looking for attention."

Will you just shut up?!

At thirteen, I'm being shuffled from one activity to another during my spring break so my mother has time to herself on hers. Ostensibly it's to keep me "out of trouble." The car journeys give her time to indoctrinate me in the ways of Mom. I am desperate for some downtime. Some time with my own thoughts. Some time to sleep late on a weekend. Some time to do things I'm not scheduled to be doing. She brags to her friends about how involved I am and all that I've accomplished. Some of it is quite exaggerated. It puts me in an awkward position when they ask me about it. I either make a liar out of her, or I perpetuate the lie. Apparently, what I do is not enough. It requires significant embellishment.

I hate it. I try to sneak a catnap in the big-ass old Oldsmobile she keeps at a temperature rivaling equatorial Africa even though it's barely a sweatshirt day. My head aches and my nose hairs cement and pull on the inside membranes. She keeps talking and shakes my arm to wake me to pay attention. "You can sleep when you're dead," she says for the zillionth time in my life. If I'm not alert to her liking when she reaches a stop sign or light, she brakes hard over and over, ricocheting my brain around in its protective juices that are no match for her industry. I jolt to consciousness.

"I just want to keep house and raise a family, Mom."

"Oh, that will *never* be enough for you. You'll be bored, and it's a waste of your gifts. You have a responsibility to those."

"Then I'll raise smart, talented kids."

"I thought I could do that too." It's here she launches into a story I've heard so many times, I could recite it myself. But it's not until today, in the midst of this conversation and my teenage contrariness, that I see it as something other than a gentle story about my beginnings. *Ugh! Here we go! I should have kept my mouth shut.*

"I thought I'd stay home with you, but I was soooo bored. There was nothing to stimulate me, nothing to hold my interest, and I didn't want to hang out with housewives and mothers. These are not interesting or educated people. I called my boss and begged him to take me back. I think we were both happier."

Yeah, Mom, I was happier because I was actually with someone who wanted to be with me all day. Who enjoyed my company. Who saw me as precious. Who spent time with me.

"All you did was eat, fill your diapers, and sleep. I needed much more and so will you. It's the quality of a relationship, not the quantity."

There is no point in arguing. I let her go on. But it's with a start that I realize as she drones, this is indeed how my mother operates. She limits her time with everyone, including my father, under the notion that quality is better than quantity in relationships. I've already developed an understanding for me—that I enjoy lying in the hammock for hours on a summer day imagining with the clouds. I can't keep her frenetic pace, and I like just *being* with my friends. As an adult, now I know that mutual rest and companionable silence contribute to the bonds we share. Holding a sleeping baby is a privilege as well as a connection to the child, to motherhood, to families gone long before, and who will be long in the future. For my mother this was an anathema. She was firmly committed to making the world a better place, and to her that meant she was constantly busy *doing* something, something that had a tangible product.

My mother raised me in a time when there was no maternity leave. She was a teacher who had to resign when I was born. When she went back after begging, she replaced another woman who had just resigned to raise a family. Her choice for my childcare was the parent of a student she knew from work. Aunt Harriet and I baked on rainy days. She always let me lick the beaters, and she watched *Captain Kangaroo* with me and kissed my boo-boos. She also taught me to say names like Ribicoff and Kennedy, to my conservative mother's dismay. She is integral in many of my early memories, and much of what I did with my own children she did with me. She liked being a mom. She was attentive to me and another girl from her neighborhood. As we grew, we played with the neighborhood kids our age and waited for the older kids to return from school. It was here I felt part of a family and a community, and it was with her I had a taste of what it might be like to have siblings.

My mother's words bust through my contemplation: "You will follow in my footsteps. You're far too intelligent to be wasting your time keeping house and wiping noses. You'll go to college and graduate school and have a career that brings meaning to your life in ways that these things can't." She is met with stony silence. Fortunately, the drive to the next activity is a short one. I get out and slam the door. She drives off, relieved of her mundane duties, to go tend to other people's children.

Sullivan and Shea

A bachelor's degree was quite unusual for women in 1924. My grandmother was in the first class in her nursing school that was able to pursue a program to earn a BSN. She was very proud of this. A quiet pioneer, she cared for the dying long before the formal hospice we know now. She always asked for the terminal patients and often worked two or three shifts in a row, tending and comforting the dying. With other patients, she asked for the sickest and the scared, and worked nights to provide assurance and comfort, sometimes stealing from the pantries of the wings built and stocked for the priests and bishops in her Catholic hospital. It was not too much to ask that she committed this sin to procure ice cream from what she termed "the gold coast" to soothe a fiery throat or help recall a pleasant memory. After her shift, she would spend time on her knees begging God's forgiveness for her venal sin.

Hers was a life of service. She served her god and the men around her: her father, her brother, her husband. At best, they took advantage of her; at worst, they abused her physically and emotionally. She took great care in her service to them and to my mother. She was a competent but cold parent, an exemplary nurse, a steadfast friend, a long-suffering spouse, a stolid Irishwoman, and when the time came, a spectacular and subversive grandparent. It seems in the latter part of her life she lived vicariously.

She taught me many things a grandmother of the fifties might have taught a granddaughter. She taught me to crochet, tat, embroider, make soda bread and corned beef and cabbage, make a proper cuppa Irish breakfast tea, and appreciate music and nature. She taught me to bake, most especially bread and pies—her pies were legendary. She taught me about family, and sacrifice, and charity. She taught me kindness. She was the kindest person I have ever known. But her most important lesson to me began when I was very young and was repeated as often as I asked for it, which I did with great predictability. It was delivered most often in the early gray light of morning, when she desperately needed sleep, but she still responded to my constant request: "Gramma, tell me a story."

I got to sleep with my gramma when I stayed for weekends. This was a delicious treat. The story was whispered quietly under the covers. I was safe and warm, cuddled against her in our own little world, while my grandmother taught me to value myself and my gender, in a subtle but powerful manner. I believed the story for more years than I should have. It was the Thanksgiving of my eighth-grade year, across the Great Plains at the dinner table, that my mother made reference to growing up with the same story.

"You mean it's not true?"

"You still believe it?! You're so gullible." Incredulity and laughing to the point of tears ensued.

It took me a few heartbeats to reconcile the fiction, and then that it wasn't conjured just for me. The generational depth was not lost on me. The fact that I was way too old to still believe it allowed me to understand its depth and influence. I wondered if some version of it had also been told to my grandmother. The efficacy of the message was subtle but relentless. It spoke to the person Gramma was, the person my mother became, and Gramma's hopes and dreams for both of us. It was delivered with just enough truth, as all fiction should be, to be believable. And of course, who wouldn't believe my grandmother? Early in her career she had been a labor and delivery nurse, and she was my mother's nurse at the time of my birth. She was privy to all the little details that make for a good birth story.

And the story goes that on that day, my father waited in the maternity waiting room with two other fathers for news of the births of their children. Each was expecting a firstborn, and all were hoping for a son (these were the days before ultrasounds). They all had their customary cigars ready and joked and paced while they waited for news.

I arrived first, swaddled in a pink blanket and presented by my grandmother to my dad and the others. Babies weren't held by dads in those days—they were immediately sent to the nursery, whose window opened on the waiting room. They gazed at me from the window. An only girl in a boomer nursery full of anonymous boys. Next arrived Shamus, Mr. Sullivan's son. Shortly after that, Sean, Mr. Shea's son. And the three dads celebrated the births of their firstborns.

But according to Gramma, something happened in that waiting room. Mr. Sullivan and Mr. Shea began to wish they had a baby girl, so it was my father who became the celebrity of the three with his girl-child in the nursery. The boys, of course, reportedly cried too much, while my little-girl self supposedly looked around at all that was going on. The boys wouldn't take bottles, and I chowed down. The boys wouldn't sleep, and I took naps. The boys were floppy, and I held up my head. The boys didn't like anyone, and I made friends with all the nurses. And so it went, until newborns and mothers were released to our homes to celebrate with our larger families.

Before leaving the hospital, Mr. Sullivan approached my dad to ask if he would like to trade babies. Mr. Sullivan thought he would prefer to have a little girl. My dad said no thank you. Shortly after that, Mr. Shea did likewise and said that he noticed that I was such an alert and engaging baby (note: not pretty—

Gramma never included my looks in the story), and would he like to trade me for Sean. My dad said he didn't think so, and that he rather liked having the best baby in the nursery full of boys.

The story could have ended there, but my grandmother had Mr. Sullivan and Mr. Shea arriving at our house at varying intervals in my early days, asking to trade poor Shamus or Sean for a now growing girl-child. Each time my parents said no, that they were happy with their little gremlin.

My parents just had me. The only child. The only girl indeed. And to their credit in that time in history, they made sure I had tinker toys and Lincoln Logs, and Play-Doh and toy cars, and fire engines and blocks. I also had my share of dolls and tea sets and a dollhouse, and I played with all of it. I know I benefitted from it in ways that articles and studies will never codify. My mother had promised that long-ago Thanksgiving when my Sullivan and Shea innocence was shattered that she would tell the Sullivan and Shea story to my daughters if I had any. When the time came, she didn't remember the story well enough to tell it.

But my grandmother, long after the story of Mr. Sullivan and Mr. Shea had been told, was quietly coaching me on how to be more than my proscribed sex role would allow, with subtle stories and examples and great love and pride in her grandgirl. When I earned my master's degree from my mother's all-girl university (an actual legacy), late into my grandmother's life, it was she who stood when my name was called, and she who nodded as I walked across the dais at graduation. I wonder about the fictional Shamus and Sean to this day. I doubt that whatever they achieved, it would have been quite enough for my grandmother.

Early May

Mother's Day

Finding good in something so insidiously destructive was a task beyond me at the time, mired in the confusion, anger, and resentment of the situation and our relationship. It wasn't until after my mother was gone that I was able to reconcile the twinkling stars—remnants of her very self—in the vast darkness of the disease. It is those twinkles and our last exchanges that sustain me.

After church on what would be my mother's last Mother's Day, my daughters, my husband, and I visited her. The common area of the ward was packed with families doing the same. We found her easily. She was perky, freshly showered, coiffed, dressed in a blouse, slacks, and slip-on shoes, none of which were hers. We'd been unable to visit her for several weeks prior because the unit had been under quarantine due to illness. We moved off to one side of the room, found and gathered sticky institutional seats, gave hugs, and said our hellos. This is where my mother lived. From a formal living room with silk upholstery and down-filled cushions, to pleather chairs that could be cleaned easily but weren't, and no place to receive guests in private. Had I been in a public place, I'd not have sat in the seats available to us. We unpacked the now-traditional Chinese takeout, which she enjoyed with great pleasure.

During lunch she was somewhat obsessive about a news report she had seen in the past. There was no news in the unit, which she missed, even if she did not understand it. My mother had, for as long as it could be accessed all day, kept the television news on in the background no matter what she was doing. Today she was recalling Queen Elizabeth II's visit to the US. She reported as if it were current.

"The queen is visiting, you know."

"Oh, Mum, I'm so glad you told me so I can have the rosebud tea set ready!"

At this she scoffed. My mother had no use for royalty.

"Will you request an audience with her, Mom?"

"Of course not!" she responded with slight annoyance, true to form. "I don't care to make her acquaintance."

This was a long-standing issue with my mother and her notions of colonialism. She never drank tea, only coffee, because in her mind it was un-American—the Boston Tea Party, taxation without representation and all. So she was sparring with me. She was in a good mood. That was really a good day. A twinkling star.

"I'd like to ask her a question, though."

"What question is that, Ma?"

"Well, she has such lovely hats and matching gloves, I wonder how she has room to pack all of them for her trip. She never wears the same ones twice."

Despite her recollections, seemingly current to her, she was remarkably lucid that day. I wondered if she would have been like this every day if she'd gotten the kind of attention she got that morning. By the time we had finished lunch, the queen was back in Buckingham Palace, and my mother was talking about gardening.

"I'm anxious to hear about your plans for the garden this year." She even knew it was spring. She was able to chat, and her contributions were not so maddeningly repetitive as usual. She was truly happy to see us all and brightly engaged. I continued to steer the conversation to things I knew she loved and were safe for us.

"Did you remember to plant marigolds around the vegetables?" She asked about perennials she had shared with me years before, and I assured her they were well, had new growth, and were ready to burst forth.

"You always liked the blue flowers, but other colors have contributions to make to the garden, you know." I'm not clear if she remembered that I planted different things every year in an effort to rotate nutrients as she'd taught me, or if she were asking specific questions because it worked in the conversation. Even so, I felt my family relax a bit and retreat from the edges of their seats, knowing this conversation could go on a bit without rancor or accusation.

"What about lilies? Did you plant lilies?" These were twinkling stars. This was my mother, the consummate gardener. She was there with us that Mother's Day. Three generations of women. This was the most we'd seen of her in months, both literally and figuratively. We discussed how my grandmother's roses were and how to prune properly. She checked in about the specimen hostas.

There was a garden in this place, but the Alzheimer's psych unit did not face it. The windows, while they allowed sun, looked out over the hulky gray air conditioning units, and other windows on other wings of the solid, functional brick building. Oblivious to this, she was enjoying the discussion, and maybe the memories of hours spent in the sun and the rain and the mud, tending, planting, replanting, rejuvenating. We talked for some time, with her interspersing now increasingly repetitive questions. Then we settled into a contented quiet. After a bit, she asked me again to tell her about my garden. I took a deep breath, looked at Brodie, who cocked his head and blew me a kiss. Fortified with his strength, I began again. I began the same litany that I had been through, aware she retained so little information from one minute to the next and trying not to be piqued by it. But she interrupted.

"No! You already told me *that*, tell me about the bees!"

We had decided to keep bees and had been preparing all winter for our beekeeping. I had talked to her about it here and there. She apparently remembered. So I told her about the bees and all the work we had done to prepare for them, the building of the hives, the placement of water, the bee suits.

"That's so exciting! They are good for the garden. You'll have more and better vegetables and blossoms. Oh! And the honey you can have with the queen in the rosebud tea set." She made a joke!

"I'll share honey with you too, Ma," I deadpanned back. No point in not adding more stickiness to the chairs. "We are picking up two colonies two Saturdays from now."

"How many bees will there be?"

"Well, Mom, there will be about fifty thousand."

We slipped into another short silence, then in complete innocence and bewilderedness, she exclaimed: "FIFTY THOUSAND! Oh, but Sarah, how will you find names for them all?!"

"I guess you'll have to help me, Mom."

"Well, yes, I guess I will. That is going to be a lot of work."

Critters

You always loved the little critters
nuisances to everyone else
you lived in harmony and awe
leaving food and water all the seasons
caging your bulbs
bordering with marigolds
but the mouse in the barrel of birdseed was a betrayal.
You released her behind the early blooming daffodils
where the early spring sun warmed the foundation
and kept the thawing earth soft and inviting under the leaf mulch
she squealed in distress as you transported her to her new home
and you sobbed in guilt and sorrow when you discovered
opening the barrel days later to scoop more seed for the critters,
her three cold curled entwined motherless babes

Window Boxes

My mother was always this way, though I wouldn't recognize it until the disease changed her and she wasn't. Isn't that how it works? My dad always quoted the proverb "You never miss the water till the well runs dry." It was also a song sung by the Ink Spots he used to listen to, and my mother used to sing to me. But it's more than a lack of perspective or understanding. Sometimes you're so busy living in your own world you don't notice. There was a lot I didn't understand about my mother then because I didn't pay attention.

She always needed time to herself, time to regroup, recoup, and regenerate because people wore her out. They didn't make sense to her. Recognition of that didn't come until I had a daughter just like her: a daughter who enjoyed people but needed time away from them. Being with others was, for both of them, an exercise in perplexity. Even after my mother was gone and I recognized the need for being alone in my daughter, even then, it was a time before I figured it out.

They were clever, the two of them: observers. They knew us well enough to know how to move in and out of our social machinations, to appear easily integrated while internally uncomfortably isolated. They were adept at finding things that made them included and simultaneously separate.

For my mother, it was the garden, and it started with the lilies. She could talk gardens and lilies with anyone. She shared and traded with friends and garden clubbers. Back in the mid-sixties, when she couldn't afford to buy lilies, she kept a shovel in the trunk of our car. I would be in charge of spotting them and Queen Anne's lace on the side of the road and alerting her. We would stop, and she would dig some up and transplant them at home, spending hours carefully separating tubers and nestling them lovingly into rich earth, each with a bit of bone meal for sustenance.

Later, when we had the resources, she would begin ordering beautiful specimen lilies she tended with the same love and care and admired with great affection. She was especially fond of Stargazer lilies with their deep velvety fuchsia centers and pure stark white edges. I could identify the different varieties by name as a child, but not because I spent time with her in the garden. My mother spent lots of time with me doing things, including planting my own garden, making gingerbread men, and playing piano duets, but her garden was time she took to herself.

She helped me start my own garden in the spring of my kindergarten year. We planted vegetables and herbs, columbine, and Queen Anne's lace. I was especially adept with radishes and herbs, which made their way to our table most summer evenings. She taught me how to weed, when to thin, and how to afford tender care to each plant, allowing the best opportunities for growth. She expressed great pleasure in my successes, and she didn't mind that my radishes were nestled in among the columbine and parsley. She taught me how to dig up things I liked and transplant them. "He who transplants, sustains," she would intone. *Qui transtulit sustinet.*

I learned about all sorts of things during our gardening. We talked about planting things to attract bees so we would have a high yield, which led to my first lessons in sex as Mom pulled apart a violet to show me male and female parts. Who knew? I chattered freely with her there. She listened carefully to my musings, asked questions, and listened again, ever the teacher. She paid attention. The blue flowers (my favorite color) showed up magically, and the daffodil bulbs (my favorite flower) arrived in time for my birthday.

It wasn't just my desires she paid attention to; there were many chats in those gardening times when her questions helped me define who I am. My mother didn't reveal much about her inner thoughts and desires; in fact, she thought it was none of my business and said so when I asked. So much so, I've probably over-shared with my own daughters to send the pendulum back in the other direction, because I wanted so much to know. As my adolescence came, mutual gardening times were fewer as other priorities —band, field hockey, and of course, friends—commanded my attention. Mom planted blue perennials in the bare spots my annuals left and just like that, the gardens survived my neglect.

My mother never refused me if I were to accompany her to her gardens, but she never encouraged me either. She worked silently and as though she were alone. I would leave after a time, not understanding companionable silence, though even that was not what she sought.

She did share her gardens with us—she gave our family famous "tours of the estate" as she called them, where I got a window on her efforts and the fruits of her labors. She would point out the lilies, violets, my grandmother's roses. She would tell us where she would be pruning next and why. She indicated how she fed, nurtured, and propagated each in its own way. We would be astonished at her accomplishments as she grabbed my father and me and led us through the paths and patches and pointed out what was new and what flourished in our backyard borders. We'd stroll as though we were royalty, who I'm not sure had flowers or gardens so beautiful as my mother's. We would delight in all of it because my mother was an artist—because her joy was infectious. She painted with her flowers on the canvas of our yard and brought colors and beauty to us, and sustenance to the little critters she enjoyed seeing in there.

These critters she fed and watered faithfully at the border edges and encouraged to visit with her plantings long before it was the thing to do. They knew a good thing. Critters would come like the monarchs to the milkweed or the hummingbirds to impatiens, surprising her with their interest. She would lovingly pot annuals at the end of summer and bring them inside along with wounded monarchs to live out their days or weather out the winter in regulated heat and humidity, only to return them as soon as possible to be with the assortment of flora inclusive of the ever-present lilies.

And my mother, who could not wait to be reunited with them, would come home from work as a psychologist in late winter and head out for an hour or two, coming back when it had become midwinter dark. Or on a Saturday, she'd be in and among the weeds and soil with the flowers and beauty that never talked back and whose needs were uncomplicated and readily met. She would come in the house dirty and sweaty and disheveled and exhausted and content with herself, with the world, with her creations, and with us. Then early Saturday night she would spend soaking in a tub, letting the dirt rinse from her cheeks and float away from under her fingernails. Alone to renew and rejuvenate.

As time went on, the sixties merged into the seventies and my high school years, and gardens and gardening became one of two consistently safe topics for discussion with my mother. Our political, social, and professional opinions were polar, and we were both passionate and smug about being right.

"When you reach maturity, you'll be a Republican," she'd declare, or "You won't be a true musician until you play jazz." And the one that really stuck in her craw, "When you have a real home, you will have a *formal* dining room with Lenox china, not *pottery*."

Those were some of the many jabs indicating I had fallen

short in my thinking and would never reach her level of competence unless I were her carbon copy. But we respected each other's space in the garden and enjoyed our parallel play.

Mother's Day was a marker for when our neck of the woods in New England was considered safe from killing frost. Mom was always excited with new plants and bulbs for a gift. We would talk flowers and vegetables. I'd marvel at her thriving blooms; she at my harvest around the seasons. We sought each other's advice on how to get the best from our gardens, whatever they held, and liberally shared the fruits of our labors, as well as tips and tricks.

My mother never came to my home without flowers, and I never went to hers without herbs and put-ups. When I became a mother, she began the tradition of the great Mother's Day exchange. We'd have an early dinner gathering—often takeout—so we could go to our respective gardens and plant our treasures, later reporting to each other where things had been placed.

"I interspersed the herbs between the hostas, Mom. They're weeds anyway; they'll choke out anything that tries to take over."

"You know, I put the new lilies you gave me just next to the peonies from your grandmother's gardens. I think the contrast is beautiful."

The disease would steal this too. She would forget so many of the names of her plantings, where she put them, or how to tend to them—even the soft and gentle Stargazers. When she went out to the gardens, she would forget what she was doing and wander dangerously into the road or the adjacent preserve behind her property, unwittingly trampling the delicate plants she had so carefully tended. By the time Mother's Day of the flower boxes came, her world had shrunk to just three rooms, with little time in the outdoors.

Had I thought about it honestly at the time, I would have known it was her last Mother's Day in her own space, but what was looming was so big and so dreadful I had yet to wrap my head around it. As it were, I brought her flower boxes that I planted to go on her balcony railing and a watering can to keep them hydrated. I filled them with a few aromatic herbs, some lavender, and the annuals she loved, and I knew they would provide her a cheerful consistent display for summer. She was overwhelmed with gratitude that I had done such a thing and told me many times that she loved flowers. After a take-out dinner, I brought her back to the balcony to enjoy them. They were as if a brand-new presentation, and she looked at me with astonishment and joy. "How did you know I liked flowers so?"

Henry

The time of COVID-19 was hard on Lillie, my youngest, who was a college student and living at home to conserve resources and save money. The isolation was acute and difficult for a woman who is social and involved. Parents don't cut it at this stage of life for company when you are building a career and looking to find others pursuing their interests and dreams like you. She had made do with online classes, social media, and computer platforms that allowed for gathering. There was a lovely surprise collection of friends and family arranged by one of her friends for her COVID birthday. Long after her father and I had left the group, we heard her laughing and exclaiming and enjoying her friends.

As restrictions loosened slowly, she and her friends would gather in a local park (coincidently enough named for a woman who was an American botanist and gardener) to enjoy each other's company outside. They all sat on their respective blankets more than six feet from each other with their masks. It became a weekly thing, something for them all to look forward to as they suffered the days in isolation. The spot they chose overlooked the bay and they were able to note the coming and going of the abundance of spring and summer, and eventually the signs of the fall to come, which she reported to me regularly.

One weekend she returned home tired and sad from her excursion.

"There was a dying honeybee in the grass by my blanket, Mom. I felt so bad for him. It took him so long to die, but I stayed with him. I named him Henry the Honeybee, and we buried him under our tree."

She has since drawn his portrait. She is my mother's grand-daughter.

Orange Blossom

My children never left my mother's home without a flower arrangement she had made with them or some bouquet of posies that she had gathered for them. My mother's workshop for her florist business was her converted garage, and my girls enjoyed hours and hours there, learning about flowers and arranging and "helping" their grandmother with her tasks. It gave my mother great pleasure that they could name all manner of flowers, and she enjoyed time spent with them out there. They all loved smelling the flowers and talking about and tasting the ones that were edible. She made things with the girls around the seasons and set them up with decorations for boxwood Christmas trees and seasonal wreaths they would use long after she was gone from their daily lives. But in these years, they made them together and chatted companionably while doing so. Spring, Summer, Halloween, Advent, Christmas, Valentine's Day, St. Patrick's Day, Easter, all with their own colors and decorative doodads carefully saved from year to year.

Much like they did my mother, people tire my eldest. COVID, however, helped Helen understand she enjoys and needs the company of her peers and her family on occasion, and that she is a good and trusted friend. It must run in families. Her friends seek her out to listen and get advice. The advice she does not give. "I'm not good at it," she says. But the listening she does. My girl is the least judgmental person I know. This past weekend, she went to an outdoor mall with friends with their masks, keeping their distance. They sat at different tables around an outdoor fountain and stopped at the macaron kiosk on the way out.

My girl called to tell me how she had enjoyed the time with friends and the outdoor time in the mall full of local flora whose scents permeated the air and were reminiscent of her grandmother's gardens. This she especially enjoyed. But the best part of her day, she said, was coming home, making tea, and getting comfortable with her orange blossom macaron.

"It was so delicious, Mom. I savored it slowly. The minute it touched the tip of my tongue it brought me right into Gran's shop, surrounded by all her flowers. I wanted to tell you so you could remember too."

Yes, I guess it does run in families.

Late May

Hospice

Later in the year, I would look back over much of this time. The images that come to me in my mind's eye are haloed and obscured with smoky grays and blues, a distancing of sorts. In so many ways I felt detached from the proceedings of my mother's incarceration. Perhaps this was protection of my very self to allow me to make decisions on her behalf and bear witness to all of it without the intensity that would surely have shredded me to ribbons. Or perhaps it was the eventuality cloaked in what felt to me to be the uncertainty of the situation that was so overwhelming and insecure. Looking back through the fog, I know vagueness was my own imposition. The professionals had mostly been straight with me.

A sharp image comes to mind, though, for just a moment, along with the jarring nature of a phone call—phone calls had become harbingers of bad news. The ring announcing the call in reality wasn't jarring at all, just a simple chime on my cell. But recalling it after the sweet innocence of the Mother's Day visit blistered through my memory. It was nary a week later when officials called to let me know that my mother had been hospitalized in their tiny facility attached to the "home." She'd had a cough that Sunday, and when I'd seen her during the week, it was clear she had a cold. I had mentioned to the floor nurse that her URIs needed to be treated aggressively because her lungs had been compromised by TB early in life. But by the time the call came she had full-fledged pneumonia. A doctor had not seen her prior to that diagnosis. Thus is the nature of care in even the best of facilities when the elderly are sick and prognosis is not good.

Being admitted to the hospital was a good thing because that meant we could see her. The ward was under quarantine again. When we saw her the afternoon of the call, she was cheerful and talkative. She bantered back and forth with her granddaughters and offered many *I love you*'s. How ironic that this illness garnered her more attention than she had when she was in the memory unit. She loved chatting up the nurses and nurses' aides when they stopped in to check on her. It was probably the most extended rewarding social time for her that she had since she left home. There were no other patients in the six-bed hospital at the time. One of the nurses' aides told me she had sat with my mother in the wee hours of the previous night and they watched a televised Roman Catholic Mass and sang hymns together, with my mother holding her own on the harmonies. I am grateful for her ministrations. They say music is one of the last things to go.

She was sitting up in bed with oxygen and IVs that first day in the hospital. The girls chattered back and forth with her about nonsense, sometimes impatient with her repeated questions or confusion, but mostly accepting of what was.

I didn't know where this hazy walk was going to take me. Perhaps somewhere in all those cloudy grays and blues I did, but that would have rendered me useless to my mother. It would have bent me in half and sucked the breath from me—not all that different from what was happening to her. *My mother is in the hospital with pneumonia, but she will get better and go back to the unit, right?* She was on IV antibiotics, and yet she continued to deteriorate. By the time the third antibiotic was introduced, she was significantly less animated and she struggled to talk. Still, she was cheery when we visited, and we four girls spoke of gratitude and love.

I asked the nurse if her tubes and accoutrements could be adjusted so that she would be comfortable sleeping on her side. My mother kept trying to roll from her back, and they kept replacing her to facilitate care. This angered me, and I got into it a bit with the charge nurse in an effort to provide my mother with some comfort and relief. She calmly and professionally informed me that there would be no comfort allowed. Comfort came when hospice was involved. I didn't allow myself to know what that meant. Wrapping up a disjointed conversation with my mother as we prepared to take our leave, we exchanged kisses and hugs as best as possible given the equipment.

"Bye, Gramma, love you!"

"Bye, Gran, love you."

"I'll see you tomorrow, Mom. I love you."

"I'll look forward to it. I love you too."

"I know you do, Ma."

Hospice? Hospice?? Wasn't she going to get better so she could go back up to the unit and be isolated and ignored most of the day waiting for one of us to visit? Where was this path leading me? Where was the romantic fading away in sleep or with loved ones surrounding her at home in some distant and obscure future? Wasn't she going to improve? The doctor called again late that afternoon, the fucking phone, and let me know that they were beginning a last resort antibiotic that evening, and that if she were to respond, it should be in the next forty-eight hours. By the time I saw her the following afternoon she was in a coma and still trying to roll over to her side. I stood at her bedside with the doctor and made the decision to involve hospice, who could come at the earliest the following morning at eight. There was a measure of relief in this as I wanted her to be comfortable and it simply slayed me to watch her fight to lie in comfort, and a measure of impatience that they could not make her comfortable immediately. Relief is misleading, though. In this discussion and eventual decision there at her bedside, I experienced the first fleeting moments of clarity since all this began. We had exchanged our last "I love you." I was going to let my mother go.

Long-Distance Call

I wished to ring you today.
The ice flowers blanketing the hills
by San Elijo Lagoon were so pink
against early spring dirt and shale,
reminding me of the mountain pinks
spilling over your native brownstone walls.
And I wanted you to know

Mozart

In a relationship fraught with discord and miscommunication, my mother and I had two ways that guaranteed mutual understanding. We could always talk about gardening, plants, flowers, and propagation without hitting a flash point. As I got older, and she less content overall, gardening was a saving grace.

But music was something else altogether. I always knew how my mother felt when she sat down at the piano by the music she chose to play. It was clear when she was angry, sad, or in need of some restoration of her sense of order. *Clair de Lune* usually indicated some measure of contentment, and she often ended a workout with Chopin or Beethoven, maybe even popular tunes, which followed her initial Bach.

She had introduced me to music in utero, and my earliest memory is of her holding my pajama-ed self in our family rocker and singing me to sleep with a spiritual she had loved since childhood, one I would hear often again during the Civil Rights Movement: "Swing Low, Sweet Chariot." In later years, she joined our church choir and encouraged me to do the same. Helen had also joined after years of grabbing her grandmother's hand from the end of the pew and recessing with her as a toddler and preschooler. Later, Lillie would do the same.

My mother had already used up a fair amount of goodwill at church by the time I was plotting her incarceration. In the months before her imprisonment, she would sometimes call the church office three or four times a day, and even in succession to ask if there were choir rehearsals. The rector joked that our family should pay the parish secretary's salary because she spent so much time attending to my mother. Choir had become an all-important event for her, and she insisted, though I had painstakingly made her a calendar with only choir events on it, that "the grid on the wall thing" did not indicate when she had rehearsals.

The undercroft, where the choir room had become a home away from home over the years, three generations of us assembled three times a week to prepare for Sunday service and upcoming events. Three generations of us singing the traditional and the modern and strengthening the musical bond between us. "Undercroft" is a WASPy church word for "basement," and this one contained the requisite smells, minus the dampness. Library smells mingled in from the vast collection of music kept there, too, steeping us in tradition and history. We would warm up there on a Sunday and rehearse a bit. Then we'd vest and line up for the processional.

On the Sunday before she would lose what autonomy she had left, I arrived at her home to pick her up for rehearsal. I found her with two blouses on and struggling to decide which black pants to wear. The creep, who saw no priority in church, was asleep as usual for a Sunday and had not assisted her in this preparation, though at this point he must have known it was likely to be confusing for her. He knew I was coming and probably figured there was no need. I stuffed down my resentment and took the several minutes required to convince her that a particular pair of trousers was just fine, and that only one blouse was needed. She had blackened some of the gray hairs near her forehead and her eyebrows that morning again with marker. Not having the time to attend to that, we washed the stray marks from her face and headed to church.

My mom was singing in her last service. When we arrived, I found her music folder for her, took out all but what she needed for the service, put it in order, and helped her vest. She had some difficulty managing her hymnal and folder, so I took the latter. At one point, when I left her with the group to use the bathroom, she made her way outside and wandered the parking lot. One of the church ladies found her and brought her back to me. It took a few minutes to disabuse her of the notion she had conjured, while meandering and apparently hunting for her car, that it had not been stolen and taken for a joyride.

The choir director was intensely aware of and remarkably patient with my mother's foibles. Her fellow altos struggled. She was a distraction. Though we sang different parts, I stood with her during morning warm-up to keep her focused and mitigate her fidgeting. When the crucifer arrived and it was time to line up in two columns by height, I again broke protocol, though I am taller than she, and made myself her partner so I could help shepherd her through the processional. This was a gamble. We banana-peeled at the altar, and I would not be next to her to keep her from aimlessly wandering. I was hoping the cues of choristers before and behind her would get her back to the narthex where I would meet her and head to the gallery.

The prelude began while we left the undercroft and mounted the stairs to the narthex to be greeted by the doors wide open to the autumnal breezes and the smell of beeswax candles and incense. This time of the church year, known as Ordinary Time, is packed with familiar tunes and readings, and otherwise familiar liturgy. Though her hymnal was upside down, Mom made it singing through the processional and the banana peel to the narthex, where I met her and we negotiated another flight of stairs in her long robes on less than steady legs to the changed smells of oiled wood, brass pipes, and the familiar sternal vibrations from the organ. I stood next to her as we filed into our places in the stalls. The service went without incident as I shared my prayer book and hymnal with her. The responses she knew by heart.

When it was time for the anthem, I handed her the music, which she promptly turned upside down, and reached over to do the same with mine. No matter. The music and alto part she knew from years of singing, and the two of us sang the soprano and alto parts of the Mozart *AVC* with one voice, hands held, never taking our eyes off our choirmaster. I've not sung it since. They say music is the last to go.

June

<h1 style="text-align:center">A Reversal</h1>

SOFT AND PINK

I t had been a family affair to take me to the furniture store to pick out a new bed and bedding. I had outgrown the crib and toddler bed. This was a rite of passage, and I was excited. We were going downtown to a big department store, and after, we were going to have lunch in their restaurant that served ice cream sundaes for dessert with a cone upside down that looked like a clown. It was the height of cool to me. I chose a twin bed set with a matching dresser and nightstand, not because I liked the furniture but because I loved the tiny pink rosebuds on the sheets in the display. The blanket was a soft plush pink with a satin border that I knew I would rub against my lip and cheek when I settled myself for "quiet time" or at night in that soft pink bed.

"Don't you like the canopy bed? You can put the sheets and blanket you like on the canopy bed."

But I was certain in my choice, even though I had the sense it was a disappointment to my mother. I felt power and autonomy. Years later I would mention how nice a canopy bed would be, and I was reminded I had been given that choice. At the time it was a giddy, heady experience, and the week's wait for delivery was interminable.

I now had my own twin beds, all walnut veneer and sleek in

what we now call mid-century, with a matching nightstand and dresser, and the rosebud sheets with a soft pink blanket. *No more baby furniture, no more crib! I'm a big girl now.* The endlessness of the week of waiting for delivery was compounded by my age and the constant admonishments that having a big girl bed meant that I also had to give up my baby ways. "You can't suck your thumb anymore in a big bed!" But I would have that new luscious blanket with the smooth border and soft plush folds to add to the sense of it all.

There had been many attempts at breaking my thumb-sucking habit to no avail. It was hoped that by making me feel accomplished and older, they might avoid putting on the pepper coating every night, and I would give it up in my new big-girl digs. I was getting tired of hearing about it when they talked to me, and I was anxious to hear something more clandestine and adult in the conversations I strained to overhear at night.

I no longer sucked my thumb during the day, avoiding censure. At this point my mother was getting up several times a night to wake me and sternly pull my thumb from my mouth. "This bad habit needs to stop. You'll have buck teeth. Money doesn't grow on trees. We can't afford braces." I'd be alone in my room, all ears for the goings-on and snippets of adult conversation I could catch. If in my vigil I remained awake and heard her coming, I'd quickly pull my thumb from my mouth and put it under the covers. She would turn on the light, though, and seek it out to see if it was still wet and wrinkled, pulling it out from under me where I'd attempted to hide and dry it. I never got away with it. "Stop sucking your thumb. You're not a baby anymore. It's a nasty, germy habit!" Of course, after she left, I'd be wide awake from the disturbance, and my thumb would go back in my mouth. I would suck and rock myself to sleep, only to be disturbed again a couple of hours or a few minutes later and go through the same ritual. If she caught me rocking too, my additional directive would be "Don't do that, only retarded children do that!" *Retarded* (a horribly unfortunate word of the times) *children must be very bad; they made my mother yell.*

In the daylight hours she would explain to me that my hands were full of germs that could make me sick, that my thumb would push out my front teeth and make me "look dumb and sound stupid" when I talked, and that "retarded children lived in hospitals away from their families." "Only low-class people have children who do these things." I didn't know what "low-class" or "retarded" meant, but they definitely did not please my mother.

She might have quit while she was ahead. It didn't take long for me to find another way to self-soothe. I wasn't on a quest to annoy her. I was trying to please her by not sucking my thumb. It never occurred to me that she would be displeased. I didn't even know there was a behavior to be discovered, and that it would be even more unacceptable.

The first time she caught me, she pulled the covers off and exposed me to the cold room. *I'm not sucking my thumb, see, aren't I a big girl?!* But she started yelling at me, angrier than I had ever seen her over my thumb. I was bewildered. "What is this? What are you doing? That's disgusting! Nasty and germy! You will NOT do *that*." I was sleepy, terrified, confused, and mute. I wasn't even sure what "*that*" was, though it would become very clear as I was stripped of my pink blanket and my hand was yanked away. This was never discussed in the daylight hours.

I tried to get smarter about not getting caught. I would lie awake for what seemed like hours with the dark pressing on me, afraid to move, and then, drifting, I would seek comfort. She became more determined to break me of my habits. She redoubled her efforts at night, sneaking quietly into my room to catch me in the act. In the mornings when she woke me for school, when I was in that obscure place between a child's dreams and the reality of the beginning of the day, having heard her alarm in the sleeping distance, she would reach into my warm soft cocoon for my hands, yank them to her face, inspect my thumb, and smell my fingers. "You've been doing that *again*?! That's disgusting. Nice girls don't do *that*." Followed by a slap across the face. Crying brought additional wrath from my father. "You keep that up and I'll give you something to cry about!" he would yell from the other room, my sobs a cheese grater on his morning mood. I learned quickly my thumb was more acceptable.

Soon, I was no longer admonished, though nocturnal interruptions continued, complete with lights, uncoverings, and smellings, well into grade school. Later her intrusions would shift to other things, though on occasion she still checked my thumb, perhaps out of habit. It never occurred to me the contrast it was to her other mothering surrounding my privacy. My mother never read my journals or letters. She never censored my reading. She didn't hover over my phone calls or get into my friendships. She never came into my room when my friends were there and always knocked on a closed door. When the door wasn't closed, she stood on the threshold and requested permission to enter. She gave advice cautiously when asked and otherwise held her tongue. But she never thought anything of busting into my room and my sleep at night to share an idea, ask a question, or curl up on my other bed because my dad was snoring too loud. It wasn't until I was out on my own that I understood the glorious comfort of several successive nights of uninterrupted sleep.

Fountain Pen

The answer was always "no"
when I asked to use the pen you almost exclusively wrote with,
except for when your hand held watercolors, pastels, charcoal.
It had a ritual.
Lovingly, respectfully, unscrew, post, ponder, dip, write, unpost,
rinse, wipe, cover,
return to place.
I'd watch in awe.
You'd show it to me when asked
over and over,
handling it carefully, explaining
the soft gold nib molded to the nature of your hand.
I stopped asking when I understood, still wishing.
It was a sacred thing, a big thing:
The relationship between this pen and this woman.
My mom.
When I pulled up my chair to the big desk
me with a generic pen
we shared my grandfather's well.
Big square heavy paperweight bottom

with an ebony top that rotated to one side to reveal the small hollow
for dipping
only opening fully to be filled from the bottle.

My mother's desk a place of wonder
in usual disarray.
Sketches, articles, notes, books, cards,
teetering piles abound.
Except, on the left, all neat.
A mail tray tucked with a small blanket for the cat,
her diluted tortoise grays and white with a bit of beige
curled therein whenever you were seated.
Your familiar.
Next to the tray, the only other thing placed carefully and
consistently
on that chaos of a desk:
The Pen.
That gray marbled fountain pen
from your dad, to keep you busy
in your sickbed at fourteen.
Delivered by your mom
ever the nurse practicing sterile technique.
No one touched you
no one breathed your dirty, dirty air.

The pen kept clean, and dipped from the well he lent.
He couldn't enter to watch or teach,
or touch the paper you gave with notes, and practice, and drawings.
Not allowed.
He waved from behind her when Nurse-Mom opened the door
slipping away before she knew he was close by.
Shame enough that one of you was sick
two would be more than the family could bear.
This distance and brevity how you two weathered

the fear and shame of consumption.
The lies: "complications of scarlet fever,"
even unwed pregnancy would have been less shameful, less dirty.

Fighting to sit up and practice,
plotting against naps.
Gargling, gargling, gargling to make thin the germy mucosity
while your mom stood and watched
arms crossed, feet planted
prepared for war with her rebel-child.
But you thrived, learned,
no inflamed lungs would keep you down.
And your pen became your familiar
no kitties then; dirty, dirty.

Many was the typeface you tried,
but one became your identity.
Only Park Avenue for you ever since.
Your sword of choice.
So many letters written
papers signed
envelopes addressed.

Now it's next to a blue Milky Way twin
gifted by you to me—my own pen-bond.
Acknowledgement I carry a legacy.
When I see yours now
in its place of honor
nib thinned and cracked
gray marbling next to my own sleeping familiar
shaded silver feline,
I mourn the enormity of loss therein
The sketches never sketched

SARAH CHURCH VOSBURGH

The words never written
The thoughts left behind
Spinning-and-colliding-and-hurtling through that infinite vessel.

Pink

The freakin' omnipresent phone insists its way into my light and agitated sleep and insinuates itself into the substance of my dream. It rings a few times before I recognize its reality. It is just after five on this late-spring morning. The sun is at a perfect slant. My bedroom is bright and warm, my husband and the dog snoozing silently beside me. I can smell the lilacs from the yard, and the seasonal insects and birds are beginning Lauds.

The phone. Again. Something's wrong. "Uh-oh," I say out loud. "Hello?"

"This is Community Home calling. Your mom has taken a turn for the worse."

"I'm meeting hospice there at eight, what do you suggest?"

"Hmm. Hospice. Hmmm. Hospice is good. But if you want to be with her at the end, you might want to come now."

"How long do you think she has?"

"Hours. Maybe a day or two."

What had I done? I had let her get this far. Was it too far? Was I not quick enough? I dress, throw on clothes for the day. *I have to call work; I have that meeting today everyone scheduled around me. No one even knows about my mom. This is all happening so fast.*

But you were hoping and expecting . . . I head out the door, internal list and self-admonishment in process, armed with Brodie's kiss— a talisman against the pain the day would bring.

The arrangements had been made the previous afternoon, when my mother was in a coma and not expected to regain consciousness. The drug-resistant pneumonia had ravaged her compromised body quickly. *There's no going back now. You were gonna meet them at eight a.m. anyway. Now she can be comfortable. They must let her be comfortable.* Everything necessary had been juggled, including the rescheduling of the meeting I needed to attend at work. *They're going to finally let her be comfortable. She's going to be comfortable.* It had become a mantra. Her end had yet to be contemplated. Though now it loomed, still distantly, hours or days away, but not now.

After making the hospice decision the night before, I went home to go about keeping life ordinary for the rest of the family, and myself really. Thinking about hospice was too much to think past the decision to do it. That evening, as I am wont to do, I slept on my side. As much as I *could* sleep. How much can you sleep when you're putting your mother in hospice?

But she'll be comfortable. It's so human, stretching out in my clean, cool sheets, such a primordial thing to find a space, a position that feels comfortable, and she can't even do that now. They're so terse and adamant about her positioning. Why? Why confine an old, sick woman this way? Why not let her find what little comfort she can? They have no concern for her.

Indeed, they had little concern for my mother as a human; she was a thing to be managed. This was one of the many ways she had become objectified. The medical mechanicals, to provide maximum benefit, had to be positioned in a particular way. *THEY had to be positioned. What about HER position?* There was no compromise between my mother's comfort and the use of the machines. *It's the right thing to do. She will feel better; she'll come out of the coma. She'll be able to say her goodbyes, and I'll be with her, many hours or days from now.* I found myself once again justifying this decision about how my mother's life would end, still not really giving any consideration to the end, just to her comfort. Perhaps it was how I got by. *They're going to let her be comfortable. She deserves to be comfortable.*

The streets are remarkably busy at five thirty a.m., but I move along with speed and expediency, losing myself in the thrum of the tires on the road, to arrive at the door of the hospital in that hypnotic state, not really knowing how I got there. It's locked at that hour. I have to bang for a minute or so to get it opened by the doctor I had spoken to the day before.

Why aren't they open? Am I at the wrong door? Did they bring her to another hospital? I'm at the wrong place. I screwed this up too. I let her down. They've moved her somewhere else, and she'll not be allowed to be on her side. She's not here; you went to the wrong place. You've failed at this too.

Irrational thoughts crowd out the list of responsibilities as I anxiously bang the door. The doctor greets me, backing away a few steps, his hands wringing with apology.

"I'm so sorry. Your mother passed a few minutes ago."

Anger at the realization that I had not been there for her last moments codifies instantly, lurking large and heavy, and at the same time obscure and unreachable. The coolness of the late spring morning pressing on the back of my neck and arms does nothing to ground me. *I didn't make it. She wasn't comfortable. She was alone. She'd been with both her parents when they died, and you left her to struggle for her last breaths on her back, hooked up to machines, and uncomfortable. You weren't quick enough. You didn't make the right decision. You should have stayed with her yesterday. You let it go too far.*

"The nurses are cleaning her up and removing the equipment. You can be with her in a minute or two."

I watch as the machines lumber out of the room in hushed haste.

The damn machines, let me see my mother! What would you have done if I arrived when she was still alive? Would you have removed the fucking equipment? What then? You told me hours, even days. What the fuck?

He tells me it was a peaceful end, but no end is peaceful when you're struggling to breathe and you can't get comfortable.

"I need to see her."

"Hmm. See her, yes, in just a minute, they are preparing her."

Preparing her for what?! She's not going to prom.

When they negotiate one more of the machines out the door, I go in anyway, giving him no choice. He follows me and reminds me it was a peaceful end.

A lonely end. An isolated, uncomfortable, struggling, lonely end, and I wasn't there.

Seeing her is a full-on assault. It is The End. She's stark raving naked, as they didn't have the time to cover her after unhooking all her machines. The moment is incongruous against a backdrop of indignity, and it makes me physically ill in that clear out-of-the-blue-ton-of-bricks kind of way that leaves you gasping and grabbing for something solid as a vertiginous veil engulfs. It is then, as I am standing alone with her at the bottom of the bed, holding on to the footboard for dear life, that I feel the earth shift beneath my feet, and I wait to hit the ground, but the jolt doesn't come. I steady myself, leaning my knees against the cool hard footboard, and will myself to feel the flatness and solidarity of the floor. Now I am firmly planted, compressed, compact, and cold; a tiny rock blown into this immensity. How does a room or a body hold the enormity of death? Simultaneously, my body is stretched thin and wispy. I am in danger of breaking apart as I am sucked into a wormhole that exaggerates space and time. Weightlessness disorients me and current pressure from all sides of this vortex heightens my dysphoria. The doctor returns to report on my mother's last moments. I hear him in real time, and I wonder how he is speaking to me through the vastness of the few feet between us. He is a lifetime away as bits and pieces of images and snippets of conversation rush by me in fast-forward. In those memories that have come unbidden,

I am swimming through a thick viscous nothingness, trying to gain a foothold on something, anything, to steady myself and gain control.

My mother is seventy-something. Frail. Emaciated. Skin and bones. If she had not forgotten how to eat, she'd certainly forgotten that it was a necessity. Coaxing had yielded only minor intake. Barely sustenance level. Bones, joints, sinew, all visible through freckled pale loose tissue-papery skin that gives the appearance it would tear if you looked at it long enough. But her breasts—oh, they are splendid! So perfect and youthful. Her charm against ageing and rejection. High, tight, firm, large (heretofore fried eggs), and round, silicone-filled mounds with bubblegum pink tattooed nipples. This is the insult that shakes me to my core. A hysterical laugh rises in my belly. I shove it down. The absurdity of it. Upon reflection, it is this contradiction that is a theme for many, if not most of the ways I would see my mother for a long time afterward.

Those breasts! On a woman who taught me I was not defined by my body but my deeds and my intellect. By the woman who admonished me harshly for masturbating alone in my room as a young child. Suddenly, all naked on her back (I'd never seen her naked) and slightly reclined in her hospital bed, she is reduced to those stupid pink plastic breasts.

Her bubblegum nipples had been a bone of contention between her and the creep. The kind of cancers she had did not allow for keeping nipple skin. They could be done surgically, but only after her general breast reconstruction had healed. She had been advised they looked best when done via tattoo. He had wanted her to have them "done" as soon as possible after reconstruction of the rest of her breasts. She went through enough at the time and put it off indefinitely. He was annoyed no end. Years later, she would go on tour to the UK with her church choir. Knowing she would be dressing in a common room much of the time, she chose to have her nipple tattoos done in advance of the trip so as not to look different. "Doing it for a bunch of old ladies who couldn't care less, but wouldn't do it for me," he grumbled. She had shrugged.

The notion of death slinks in. *My mother is dead. Seventy-something years old. Young these days, my mother is still young. She should be enjoying life, her friends, her grandchildren, her gardens, her flowers. But she is dead. Dead and sexualized. Dead and objectified. Dead but in a position that allowed for wires and leads to record her vitals. Vitals—nope deadals. Dead with perfect breasts and an otherwise wasted body and mind.* "Pneumonia is the old people's friend," my grandmother the nurse used to say. But my mother was much longer dead than deadness would imply. Or vacant at least—her mind, her memories, her very essence ravaged. *She's been gone so long now. Why are you so upset about this? You knew those breasts were there. You knew she wasn't. Why does it bother you?*

My mother, whose Catholic high school dark-of-the-night hijinks consisted of placing an unlit cigarette in the uplifted hand of the statue of the Blessed-Virgin-Mary-Mother-of-God and painting her exposed toenails red for the student body to pass in lines on the way to early morning holy-day-of-obligation Mass the following day.

My mother, to whom everyone bared their soul. She was a faithful, steadfast, loyal, supportive, and ever available friend. She told no tales, violated no secrets. She willingly and graciously accepted foibles and quirks and stood by through sick and sin.

My mother, whose love affair with her guns and her second amendment rights cost her opportunities for time in her own home with her grandchildren. It cost them too—that escape to Grandma's, the unconditional love coupled with the undivided time and uninhibited adoration.

My mother, who taught me to sew, and paint, and draw, and love music, and write, and study, and learn, and love, and be a friend, and be modest. *Look who's modest now, ha! Bubblegum nipples. Seriously?* Who taught me about loyalty and commitment and honor and values and morals and trustworthiness. Who also taught me to lie and trust no one. Who taught me that I was a disappointment. *Not quick enough. Not smart enough. Not talented enough. Not ambitious enough. That should be my epitaph. Here Lies Someone Who Was Not Enough.* My mother, from whom I had to wrest my psyche when I was wrapped in the clutches of her insecurity. My mother, who needed so much validation for her own opinions and choices that it led to forcing them on me or belittling me when I chose a different path.

My mother, who couldn't cook but loved to eat. Who struggled to love but loved to be loved. Who nurtured those at a distance more than the ones close to her, and who kept her feelings and hurts to herself. My mother was so much more than this absurd pink pair of plastic breasts.

Who will teach me now? Who will listen now? Who will murmur now? Who? Who will name the bees?

Mind Over Matter

A determined one she was, my mother. Not much stood in her way of living. Very little laid her low. Like the little engine that could, or the pink bunny, she just kept going. If she had a bug, she just carried on (spreading her germs wherever she went) and took whatever medications were prescribed for her. If my mother missed work or ended up horizontal, it was cause for serious concern. I could count on the fingers of one hand the times it happened over the years.

When her thumbs were bothering her from degenerative arthritis, the hand surgeon bellowed at her, "Why didn't you come see me sooner? I could have fixed this so much earlier. There is no need for you to be in this kind of pain." It was clearly not always a wise thing that she functioned in this fashion.

Some of it stems from the times in her teens when she had tuberculosis. My grandmother was mortified by this. Only dirty people got TB. Rather than send my mother to a sanatorium where she might have been with other dirty teenagers, she talked the doctor into allowing her to treat my mother at home, because she was a nurse and could tend to my mother properly and observe sterile procedure. My grandmother had a reputation for extreme competence. No one was to know, and if my mother's health were asked after, folks were told she was recovering from scarlet fever at home.

My mother would probably have had less confinement and more interaction in a sanatorium. For a year she saw only the four walls of her bedroom, the tiny bathroom across the hall from her, and my grandmother. She took her meals in her room and otherwise occupied herself there. She did not see my grandfather for much of that first year, because he was so terrified of contracting the disease, he would not even poke his head in to say hello. My mother's friends knew nothing except that she needed rest and they couldn't see her. I'm surprised everyone didn't think she'd been sent away to a home for unwed mothers. Maybe they did.

It was during this time she decided determinedly that she would not sleep anymore unless she absolutely needed it, that she would not spend any unnecessary time in her bedroom, and she would stop for nothing once she was out of the woods. She learned from bed how to do calligraphy, she read all the *Nancy Drew* mysteries, she sketched, drew, wrote letters, painted, and fought her mother over every restriction. She would study and take exams from bed (which was unheard of at the time), and the Mother Superior from her Catholic school allowed her promotion with the rest of her class, which was also unheard of.

She went back to school the following fall, only to be pulled out one more fall later, in high school. She was told she had it again. We now know it is likely she never got rid of it the first time, and it just lay in wait to gather strength to lay her low again. The second time she had it, she was a test case for a new penicillin and recovered with remarkable speed. There was still the requisite endless period of clear X-rays when she was allowed no visitors or activity.

It is not surprising, having had these experiences, that my mother would adopt a mind-over-matter attitude about illness. To her, there was no illness one couldn't overcome if one simply availed oneself of modern medicine and had the determination to do so. It was how she survived cancer, joint replacement, and hysterectomy (recovering in record time, of course).

She had marginal patience for me being sick, and she encouraged me, if I needed to be home, to remain busy, or "at least read" so as not to waste the time. She made me canned chicken soup, beef consommé, or tea and toast as my sick foods. The one thing for which she had no patience was menstrual issues. Suck it up, buttercup.

"You may not be less-than one or two days out of every month. This is the kind of behavior that keeps women down." If you asked her if she were a feminist, she would have said no.

But my mother met her match in Alzheimer's. I'm fully convinced that she knew she had it from the beginning, and she decided grit and determination would prevent it from getting the better of her. I'm convinced it is what allowed her to pull herself together in many a social situation for years, and what allowed her to develop generic statements that wouldn't raise eyebrows in conversation and kept her integral for so long. Back before she had it, she worried about her *final exit* and bought a book with the same title with instructions for ending things if she felt it necessary. She was hell bent and determined not to be a burden on me. We fought over this. I was prepared and willing to care for her. Little did I know I needn't have worried, as the disease took these "choices" from her.

A few months before my mother left home, she had her first and only seizure, which is common in about 20 percent of dementia patients. The creep had called us, and then 911, to get her to the hospital. We met them there, and we stayed with her, while he went home to be ready for her when she got there. She was given medication that made her kind of Gumbyesque in mind and body, and it was my husband who got her into the car and sat with her in the back seat so that she didn't crumple and hurt herself. During the ride she mistook my husband for hers, referring to her son-in-law by her husband's name.

"I don't want to be a burden to Sarah; you have to take care of me like you promised." My husband assured her he would do just that, and he did. The creep just got more and more frustrated with her.

I know in my heart of hearts that my mother heard and understood the conversation with her doctor at the end of her hospital bed when we decided hospice was the best course of action. I know she plotted in her head how she would be the least burden. She chose to "spare" us and died in her own time, on her own terms, as her parting gift to a grieving family.

Sing Me to Heaven[1]

In my heart's sequestered chambers
lie truths stripped of poets' gloss;
Words alone are vain and vacant,
and my heart is mute.
In response to aching silence,
memory summons half-heard voices,
and my soul finds primal eloquence
and wraps me in song.
If you would comfort me, sing me a lullaby;
If you would win my heart, sing me a love song;
If you would mourn me and bring me to God,
sing me a requiem, sing me to Heaven.
Touch in me all love and passion, pain and pleasure
Touch in me grief and comfort, love and passion,
pain and pleasure
Sing me a lullaby, a love song, a requiem
Love me, comfort me, bring me to God
Sing me a love song, sing me to Heaven.

---

1. "Sing Me to Heaven," Composer, Daniel E Gawthrop; Lyricist, Jane Griner; Dunstan House, 1991; Choral work for SATB acapella.

Sing Me to Heaven

The creep wanted no part in planning my mother's funeral, despite our attempts to involve him in choices. I worried this would bite me in the ass at some point, as he was her husband and it was largely his place to orchestrate it. But it wasn't any different from any of the other decisions that had been made over the last year. He called me, expected a fix, and sat in the corner wringing his hands, sobbing, and bemoaning his changed life. When it was all over, this wasn't what bit me. It would be the call two weeks after she died asking for the check for his inheritance: "I need to move on."

Despite our honest and kind efforts at inclusion in *any* decision or participation during the past year or her funeral, he refused to do a reading, make choices which were offered, or take part in the service at all. He spent the hour-and-a-half service blubbering next to me and the granddaughters. The rest of us took part in some way. I spoke on my mother's behalf, my husband was the chalice bearer, both the grandchildren did readings, and the eldest was a pallbearer. There had been an ordination just hours before and the parking lot and parts of the narthex had remnants of red confetti. The presence of the Holy Ghost.

There were no flowers. My mother said for a lifetime that she wanted flowers when she was living, and not to bother to send them when she died. Of course, when she became a florist, it made the giving a bit more difficult, but there were always plants for the garden.

We did not sing the Mozart *Ave Verum Corpus* because the cathedral choir was on hiatus by then. On request, our precentor did the Kontakion most beautifully, and our new tenor sang "Swing Low, Sweet Chariot"—fitting, I thought. We choristers in the family otherwise picked favorite hymns and responses that she'd sung for a lifetime. Familiar, comforting, and surreal all at once. Had it been someone else's service, she'd have said it was just lovely and been content to chat up those in attendance. An ancient ritual, a human mark of passage in community. A bookend on her Baptismal Covenant (protect the dignity of every human being). As my dad would have said: She'd been hatched, matched, and dispatched. Dispatched in song, though. She had been sung to heaven.

Epilogue

Spring

Back in grade-school days when I was reading *The Hobbit* (Tolkien, 1937), I developed a love of "The Road Goes Ever On" and "I Sit Beside the Fire and Think" poems therein. They change as the story advances, and each of them spoke to me for one reason or another beyond the scope of the tale. The phrase that first captured my imagination was "when winter comes without a spring that I shall ever see."

Not one spring has passed (or the change of a season, for that matter) that those words have not echoed in my head and given me pause. Pause of a good kind. Pause that allows for living in the moment and allowing the ampleness of that moment to fill me. Indeed, I think Bilbo Baggins would be proud. I reminisce fondly also of the springs I shared with my mother, our plantings and transplantings, and our eager, impatient anticipation to see the fruits of our labors.

Spring of the year of my mother's death was an especially early one. It was likely no more beautiful than a New England spring has ever been, which is indeed spectacular. The turning of all the seasons is gorgeous in this part of the world, and a privilege to witness. Perhaps spring is the most drastic of the turnings. The other seasons seem to fade into each other, but spring enters with deliberate determined messy joy from the crisp clean starkness of winter.

When else can one experience "mud-luscious" and "puddle-wonderful" ("in just— spring"; e. e. cummings, 1927) while looking over a haze of the yellow and green lawns full of dandelions? The beginning of the seasonal put-ups come with spring. First the dandelion jelly, then pickled asparagus and a march on through the appreciation of days of picking and putting up, into high summer with the onset of plenty. My mother's flowers and shrubs planned for flowering in succession were in full joyful display.

Having lived in these parts since birth, my mother had pointed out the daffodils at a local park, the *Muscari* that carpet the lawn at a city college, the hazy red blooms that give way to early greens of the maples and signal the end of sugaring season, the planned serial displays on the sprawling lawns of insurance campuses, the heartiness and cheeriness of the pansies sold by the flower lady on the corner by the cemetery in very early spring, and the joy of the shoots of all manner of plants that poke through year after year. We even altered and lengthened our routes by season, Mom and I, to have the chance to revel in the beauty a bloom has to offer. How is it then that we somehow missed the blooming of the fruit trees in the local orchards?

For all the years that I've lived and worked nearby, and for all the years that I have picked fruit and vegetables at a local orchard, it wasn't until she was dead that I drove through the orchards while the fruit trees were in naked bloom. Why had my mother and I never done this? It is stunning. Miles and miles of pink and white fog across the rolling hills. Before too long there would be a carpet of pink and white petals beneath the fresh green of the emerging leaves and buds on those trees.

"Without a spring that I shall ever see" takes on new meaning. Neither I nor anyone else knows how many springs we will see or how many springs we will share with a loved one. But I know I will not be here to witness the slow, steady, relentless, abundant beauty of the march from winter to summer in my mother's gardens or my native New England again anytime soon. I hope I will bear witness to a different spring that will carry with it a host of new discoveries about that very same progression. Would that I could share my new discoveries with her. I will hold the fullness of my mother's gardens and the New England spring in my heart, as it has indeed become a part of who I am.

Qui Transtulit Sustinet

It had poured all night, and the rain now is light and steady. The morning air is laced with petrichor, and the brightness of the fallen yellows, oranges, and reds is stark and sharp against the grayness of the day. A bit over a year since she had last been home. It was the kind of day one would be likely to find my mother up to her elbows in mud, thinning and transplanting in her gardens to allow plants to settle before their dormancy. This was the perfect kind of weather, soil density, and time of year for such cultivation. As it were, her friends were coming to dig in her gardens and gather specimens my mother had cherished and nurtured for their own gardens. This day had been planned on the day of her funeral when someone had asked if she still had apricot-colored violets in her garden, and would I be willing to share. He who transplants sustains.

They come with their trowels, kneepads, and clay pots, one by one, or in groups, with a hushed sort of reverence. While waiting on the three-season porch with hot cider and extra pots and the memories of years past when I'd left soups and lavender for my recuperating mother, or when Lillie with her halo of blonde ringlets would stand on tiptoe to ring the doorbell to see her Gran, once in a while I hear a whoop as someone finds something they had either given her or divided up with her, with an accompanying call to others to come share in the bounty. I hear many stories that day, some familiar, some new, about the garden club or particular plantings she had done with friends. Many tell me of plantings in their own gardens that had already come from my mother who reveled in making gardeners out of her friends. The garden club ladies came the most prepared, with their aprons and gardening pants pressed perfectly with a crease and reinforced knees. They look as though they'd walked off the cover of *Better Homes and Gardens*. My mother was a bit envious of them in her day. She never was able to maintain a pressed and polished look while gardening (or ever, really), nor did she try, but her appreciation for those who did and could was unbounded.

A light icing is predicted for late afternoon, and as the day grows colder, the digging stops. The stories and camaraderie do not. They gather on the porch and share and laugh and take long looks around at the appurtenances my mother had placed for comfort and joy around her three-season room. This was her favorite place, along with her library. When the temperature drops and ice threatens, in an effort to avoid treacherous conditions on the way home, they take their leave.

I stand alone.

One of the first memories I have of that porch is waking my mom on a deep midsummer night to share with her the reflections of a full moon on our world. Both of us out there in our bare feet on cool flagstone, marveling at the beauty of the blue light cast on our familiar trees and fences and blooms. We'd do the same in midwinter to see the moon reflect silver on the snow. Other nights we would stand there silently and listen to the distinct but indescribable sound of falling snow.

This evening, with friends and family gone, the house locked and ready for the real estate agent on Monday, and the porch at rest, I head out, waiting for the slam and click of the wood-framed screen door, and am greeted not by the predicted ice but big flakes of a light snow. I stop to listen and know she is out there.

Afterword

Only three months before the eventual incarceration, we finally succeeded in hoodwinking my mother to see a neurologist, something she had refused to do. She knew enough to know that an evaluation was going to cost her autonomy, and she'd been fighting it for years by the time we were able to get her to go. The dear friend who had found her wandering the post road months before and brought her back home was a pathologist at the university hospital. He recommended the neurologist we would see.

Our friend graciously agreed to meet my mother for lunch the day of her appointment. He made arrangements with the neurologist to meet them in the medical center lunchroom so he could casually introduce them. My mother didn't see it coming. They sat and chatted for over an hour until she was comfortable walking with her old family friend to the neurologist's office for an evaluation she didn't know was already underway. She was scheduled for an open MRI that day, but they were unable to get her to comply for very long with the directions to stay put and still. Even so, they got the information needed to make as clear a diagnosis as was possible at that time—Alzheimer's dementia.

It was no surprise to any of us.

We called the neurologist at the university the day my mother died and offered her brain to the Neurology Department. Anything to advance the science. She was grateful. The neurologist commented several times that my mother must have been a truly brilliant woman to have covered and recovered for so long, and she wished they had met in other circumstances. My mother's brain remains pickled there with my grandmother's, about which they both would have been pleased. Two generations. I fear mine will join them before too long. The rest of her was cremated and would be mixed with the remains of my father and buried per their instructions (my father referred to this as *coitus in perpetua*).

What is left, in a somewhat ethereal nature, are stories. What are our stories? What is memory, the memory that was so cruelly and inexorably extracted from my mother? Wendell Berry is attributed with the quote, "We are nothing without stories." I don't want my mother to be nothing. I don't want to be nothing. I fear the loss of self, of family stories, my stories, the leaves and twigs on the branches of our associative and collective memories. I was a helpless spectator as my grandmother, and later my mother, lost their stories, memories, and their very essences to Alzheimer's, leaving a once proud family tree full of memories without branches, leaves, or even twigs. And they were helpless spectators when my great-grandfather was likewise afflicted. The stories herein I've inherited along with my own experiences to share forward.

My mother's stories, her love, her memories, tangle with mine, strong vines of memories green, lush, entwined. Hers with my grandmother's, and mine with my children's. They go on as leaves and twigs and intertwined branches on a storied old tree. Each retelling augments strength and richness of character. The vista afforded in the bloom of each generation brings a renaissance of love on display if only by virtue of someone bothering to remember and tell the stories.

I repeat the family stories. I water and fertilize and nurture the memories to ensure their life from one season to the next. My mother would lose most of her stories; the rest she would confabulate. She always said life was about learning to let go. Stories are a way to hold on with open arms.

My mother mattered. It is my gamble that I have mattered. I hope my contribution has been a good one, which has helped sustain memory, identity, and family. That I have remembered my mother in all her messy wonder. That by my actions, my storytelling, I have loved my mother. That day-to-day tacit love, spoken aloud in stories, has been enough to sustain us both.

Under the sheets by early morning light, in the crook of warmth cuddled next to my grandmother, I began to love real stories.

"Gramma, tell me about when Mommy was born."

"Again? You know that story by heart, and Grampa told it to you last night!"

"Tell it again, Gramma, pleeeeease."

A serious and anxious child in anxious times—Khrushchev banging his shoe at the UN, Bay of Pigs, my president dead, the Cold War—I listened with unwavering attention, hanging on each adult word, noticing when tones changed and body language stiffened. Drifting away into the "olden days," I found respite from the apprehensions of my own time, imagining when my forbears were little like me and lived what I thought to be a simpler, safer life.

I am well aware I come to this Alzheimer's game from a place of privilege. Though I was a generation sandwiched between children to raise and an elderly parent who needed as much if not more care than the children, I am acutely aware I had a privileged upbringing and resources available to me. I did not do this alone, and though the help I needed (and my mother needed) at times was unavailable, I spent much time wondering how families manage this without resources. Those very resources allowed me the energy to preserve the memories my mother could not. For any of us, when it comes right down to it, the protracted loss— watching the fading of a life, of a person, of an essence—is painful, exhausting, torturous at best. Later, when the body rests and maturity tempers, there is both sweet sorrow and joy simultaneously holding gratitude and awe for a life well lived and the remaining stories rich and steeped in love.

This book is memories of love unspoken, and oft times unfelt. This is a daughter's love letter in which abiding, wordless, but resonant love of a mother is recognized and returned with new fullness. It is raw, exposed layers of memory and oral history through acts of brutal necessity and tender love in the history of years and the waning months of a life rich and deep. It includes the poignant and the perturbations. There is no whitewashing here. We are who we are, and I, for one, would like to be represented as who I was in all my contradictions if anyone cares to speak of me after I'm gone. I realize, much like artwork, our actions, words, and very selves are different things to different people. We've little control over how others see us, or how our intentions are interpreted. That said, there are truths. I have come to know I am worthy to tell our stories, to embrace our memories, and our truths herein.

As the years ensue, I've forgiven my mother my notions of her failings, betrayals, and her unavoidable decline over which she had no control (not for her lack of trying). I can now recognize she was the best mother she knew how to be. Beyond that, there is the richness and depth of herself that she shared with me: her flowers, music, art, and love. An imperfect yet complete love I was unable to recognize as it was given.

I quote her often now. Mostly about life. Some quotes were from things she'd read, though more often than not, they were her own musings that codified over the years. Her wisdoms. The wisdom I didn't recognize right along with the love. Some second-generation quotes she brought forth from my grandmother—maybe it was the same for my mother. "You never miss the water till the well runs dry."

This is a legacy I would prefer not to pass on, though I'm beginning to think it's an inescapable facet of the human condition. I watch my daughters and feel their lack of understanding of my decisions or actions, and know that only time, distance, and the knowledge gained in the death of a loved one can bring focus.

If ever you asked me in any of the years before my mother's death if she loved me, I'd have responded with an unequivocal "Yes," even as a miserable tween, though I did not fully understand why I even said it. Perhaps I wasn't meant to understand, just to have faith in my mother's love in all its imperfection. It might have overwhelmed a younger daughter to know the breadth and depth of it. Now though, in fragments and pieces, I grasp the edge of its fathomless unconditional nature, even as I am absolutely sure of my love for my own daughters.

I often, but briefly, hold in my heart the well-forged and tempered distinctive brand of love that belongs to my mother and me. It is ours and ours alone. It threatens to burst my soul, and I hold it gently, but steadily with awe, and reverence, and love. *And the greatest of these is love.*

Acknowledgments

Writing never came naturally to me; this story, this memoir, is something that found its way to paper by necessity of love and grief. Over the years, my writing teachers had been unimpressed, and one wrote in my yearbook, "You should be *okay* if you meet your deadlines." Thanks, Mrs. Ellis. I kinda like that whooshing sound deadlines make when they go by. To B. H. Lowell, and A. G. Drosselmeyer, a hearty thanks for planting that tiny, silly seed of a notion. There was a time I gave fleeting thought to writing and illustrating picture books for children, but I did not pursue it and never gave a nanosecond of synaptic time to the notion of writing fiction or nonfiction for adults. Nevertheless, in halcyon days at the lake each summer, reciting poetry on deck or dock, or lying on the dock on our backs in the middle of Perseid meteor showers, these two friends and I, with all twenty-something cheek and great hilarity, invented ridiculous titles for our future tomes. Only one of us was likely to write one, and it was not me.

It takes a village to make an author, and I'd not be one were it not for San Diego Writers, Ink and the International Memoir Writers Association. There, I was given the opportunity to study the craft and mature in skill. Special thanks to W. Fulkerson, T. J. Jones, M. Freedman, C. de los Ríos, and T. Pryputniewicz, who all had a hand in getting me started.

Those who kept me going (and going) were the Read and Critique Writeous Sisters. Never fearful of the critique part, as my expectations were low, I became a member, and The Sisters loaded me up with constructive criticism, laughs, tears, trust, and examples of the *most spectacular and inspiring* writing. My love, awe, and gratitude (in no particular order) go to: T. J. Jones, D. Rudell, L. Ferguson, J. Gasner, L. Cross, L. Engel, I. Bowers, K. McLane, K. McCabe, S. Esmail, S. Gold, M. Balacek, S. Jones, A. Mautner, and M. French. Thank you for making a safe place where we could all be vulnerable, grow, and learn.

Friends and colleagues over the years shared stories of my mother with me, or helped my mother through challenging times, others listened when I told stories and asked for more, and some reminded me of details or asked questions that brought more to light. Still others listened to or read first drafts of sections, or shared their own writings with me, and all encouraged me to persevere. Each has, in their own unique way, been integral to this process. Again, in no particular order goes my love and gratitude to: E. L. V. Civitello, M. P. Kester, A. Breakstone, J. Tsutsui, A. Strickland, L. C. Kehlenbach, E. Gangaram, R. & S. Nocera, D. H. B. Borton, D. L. Lenehan, K. Mercado, D. Scherling, L. L. Lorenson, A. Allen, D. S. Downes, S. J. Hickson, N. M. Heckler, P. S. Checko, K. H. V. M. Midney, L. L. D'Arcangelo, C. Harlow-Jennings, P. A. Reasoner, K. Cameron, S. L. Jensen-Bradley, J. L. C. & R. M., M. Jesperson, D. Boruch, C. H. Martin, A. Defilio, Becky F., L. B. R., J. Bryson, L. MacDonald, K. B. Davis, M. W. Davis, L. F. Sierra, R. H. B., G. Desrochers, and D. Harris.

R. H-D, who made a point to attend my first reading after my first story was published, where the authors outnumbered the attendees: Your warm heart, faith, and encouragement brighten my days.

In the crescendo of this journey, there are the folks at Acorn who believed in me and my stories. They took on overwhelming tasks and details about which authors are often clueless (you just write the book, right?), guiding me through. Much gratitude goes to H. Kammier, N. Seidita, and K. Ross, who each set me straight more than once—and had confidence in me during the whole project. Thank you too, MK Conway, for social media savvy that simply escapes me.

Without my family, none of this would be. They supported

me through the events, the memories, the tears, the sadness, the frustrations, the joys, and the laughter. So many layers, so much support from: A. S. Boyer, J. E. Plourd, L. E. Vosburgh, H. K. Vosburgh, and my champion of champions, my husband, B. S. Vosburgh. He put up with my nighttime musings/writing, reading, and rereading, attending to what I neglected because I was writing or crying into the fur of my feline extraordinaire out of frustration, abject imposter syndrome, or unmitigated grief.

Last but decidedly not least, thank you, readers. A warm welcome to the hive.

About the Author

It was never in Sarah Vosburgh's plan to be an author or to write a memoir. As a busy mom, wife, and psychologist, she always saw her life as full (sometimes overfull). But in the dark of night, memories knocked on her brain, compelling her to commit them first to paper, then to bits and bytes.

Sarah is a member of the International Memoir Writers Association and San Diego Writers, Ink. Her work has been published in *A Year in Ink* and numerous volumes of *Shaking the Tree: brazen. short. memoir.* A native New Englander, she now lives in San Diego with her husband, daughter, granddog, and a most extraordinary feline.

Sarah can be reached and resources can be found at:
www.SarahVosburgh.com